CONCILIUM

Religion in the Seventies

CONCILIUM

Concilium 115 (5/1978): Fundamental Theology

DOING THEOLOGY IN NEW PLACES

Edited by
Jean-Pierre Jossua
and
Johann Baptist Metz

A CROSSROAD BOOK
The Seabury Press · New York

1979
The Seabury Press
815 Second Avenue
New York, N.Y. 10017

Library of Congress Catalog Card Number 78-71627
ISBN: 0-8164-0394-5
ISBN: 0-8164-2611-2 (pbk.)
Printed in the United States of America

CONTENTS

PART I

New Contexts of Theology

Karl Derksen

Non-university Theology in the Netherlands

I WILL not attempt to define precisely what is meant in this article by non-university theology, although the meaning may perhaps be clearer by the end. The fact remains, however, that there has never been a lack, in the Netherlands at least, of individuals and groups practising theology outside the theological faculties, colleges or seminaries. This non-academic theology has often been done—and is still done—by, or is at the service of, movements that want their own view to be presented within or on the periphery of the great Christian denominations. This phenomenon is more easily discernible within the Reformed tradition in the Netherlands than within the Roman Catholic tradition. It is much easier for a new and verifiable subject of faith (a church community, movement or modality) with its own theology to emerge within the Protestant tradition. It is only in recent years that very divergent groups have also arisen within the Roman Catholic community of faith. The Dutch saying can now be applied to the whole Christian people of the Netherlands: one Dutchman is a theologian, two Dutchmen are a church and three are a schism.

In this article, I leave the more distant past out of account and confine myself to examples of non-university theologies that have been produced in recent years. I will describe these briefly and place them in the context of what has been going on in the Dutch churches and in Dutch society.

THE NINETEEN-SIXTIES

If we confine our attention to the Roman Catholic community of faith in the Netherlands—in the long run, differences that were not strictly confessional were to play a part in Christian life during this period—we notice that the nineteen-sixties were marked by the publication of the *New Catechism* (the Netherlands, 1966; Britain and America, 1967, where it became popularly known as the 'Dutch Catechism'). This was also the time when Catholic thinking was set in motion in connection with the Pastoral Council of the Dutch province of the Church (1966-1970). In both instances, a non-university theology was involved. The original concept of the *New Catechism* was the work of professional theologians, but the final text of the book was decisively influenced by the ten thousand comments made by a hundred-and-fifty people. Thousands of discussion groups were active in influencing the various commissions of the Dutch Pastoral Council in their preparation of texts as were the letters received from countless individuals. The Dutch Catechism and the Pastoral Council in this way became the deposit of the way in which many Dutch people felt about their faith. The inspiration of these two factors led to a spread of theological reflection among people other than professional theologians and those holding office in the Church. It seemed as though the whole of the Dutch Catholic Church wanted to practise *aggiornamento,* and precisely for this reason a conservative counter-movement emerged in the Church. The group known as 'Confrontatie' was originally formed in 1964 to keep a careful guard over the impulses generated by Vatican II, but as time went by it became, together with several other similar groups, increasingly fanatical in its accusations against the Pastoral Council. A process of democratization in the structures of the Church which had just been set in motion and an increasing openness in theological thinking were called seriously into question and not only by the conservative groups. By now, it was 1968.

1968

Although I would prefer to avoid mystifying the year 1968, it would indicate a great lack of historical feeling on my part if I ignored the decisive importance of that year, not only for society as a whole, but for Christian theory and practice. Paris 1968, Prague 1968, Medellin 1968 and Uppsala 1968—these are all expressive of ideals and dreams that are still having an effect today. New Christian groups began to arise in that year in the Netherlands. A new solidarity was felt within monastic communities, theological faculties and Church communities, in an attempt to make it even clearer in word and deed that the gospel message was liberating. Taking various forms of lack of freedom in the Church as their point of departure (priestly celibacy, for example, and Catholic moral teaching about marriage), Christians soon became aware of the connections between structures and ideologies in society and those in the Church. A group of theologians connected with the journal *Tegenspraak* drew attention again and again to these connections. They were inspired by J. B. Metz's political theology and were in contact with similar groups in other countries (the group known as Kritischer Katholizismus in West Germany, for instance). Radical questions were asked about the process of adaptation that was taking place within the Dutch churches, such questions as, for example, were the churches aware that the process of democratization and the indiscriminate and triumphant application of the findings of the modern human sciences to theology simply added strength to late capitalist structures and ideologies?—what did the Church and theologians think of such phenomena as the accumulation of more and more power in fewer and fewer hands?

It was also at about this time that a reduction in the number of seminaries and monastic teaching institutions (hitherto fifty) was taking place in the Netherlands, the final number being four institutions, which together with the Catholic theological faculty of Nijmegen, five faculties of Reformed theology and a number of other Reformed institutions were to take care of university theology in the future. The question remains as to whether these institutions will have sufficient knowledge and skill to have an effect on what is taking place at the basis.

THE NINETEEN-SEVENTIES

This word, 'basis', has in recent years come to have an increasingly specific meaning in the Netherlands. It has become the key-word for all theory and practice that arises from below where man, in his actual psychological and social alienation, is found. In the nineteen-sixties, there were many groups engaged in social and political action against the leadership in society. These have grown in number and strength and their members listen and are obedient to the voice of the oppressed at home and abroad.

In 1970, Septuagint, a group of priests, Protestant ministers and lay-people working in solidarity with each other, evolved the concept of critical and active communities. According to their statement, 'Such communities arise where people, because of their practical commitment to their fellow men and the world, continue to ask questions together about the meaning and the future of that event. . . . This does not mean that Churches and communities should devote all their energy to theology, pious reflection about themselves or attempts to justify their traditions and structures. It means, on the contrary, that they should not avoid questions about salvation or its absence, or thrust them aside as irrelevant, but should be practically committed to the whole human event. . . . Such communities must be critical both of themselves, their understanding of the Gospel and their own form of community life and of the historical reality in which they are situated, the views, ideologies and structures of their society and their own attitude towards that event'.

In a report published in 1972, Septuagint declared: 'It is essential for us to acquire a biblical theological insight and knowledge at a very high level. Only good theology can defeat bad right-wing theology'. This declaration was made in an even clearer form in March 1973: 'We are concerned with all those workers, lay-people and theologians who are inspired by the gospel in their commitment to society. Because of the dissemination of antiquated and wrong views about the essential teaching of the Judaeo-Christian tradition, or because of an incomplete traditional Christian upbringing, the essential elements of the Judaeo-Christian culture that originated in circles of resistance to slavery and oppression are frequently neglected. In order to enable our grass-roots workers to become familiar with those essential elements, a group will concern itself especially with a biblical theology that consciously seeks help from the Marxist view of society today'.

In the early nineteen-seventies, then, the protest movement within the Church, which consisted of individuals (and mainly those bearing office), developed quite rapidly into a 'basic' movement of groups and communities. This movement began to display its own theological characteristics in contrast to the conservative groups, the charismatic movement that was just beginning to emerge, and the centre, the members of which had hardly been able to preserve any of the early enthusiasm of the Dutch Pastoral Council of the nineteen-sixties since a decisive intervention on the part of higher authorities.

From 1973 onwards, the events in Chile and a new movement calling itself 'Christians for Socialism' within the basic movement in the Netherlands began to play an important part. This was entirely in accordance with the declaration of the International Conference of Critical Christians in Lyons in November 1973: 'We are re-reading the Gospel. We are reading it as the Word of God that cannot be understood independently of a firm will to expose oppressive systems and their ideologies—systems which our Churches all too frequently try to safeguard. This Word of God invites us to recognize him and to express him who, we believe, is today and always the living Word in our history. In Jesus Christ it was revealed to us that God is not an absolute lord and master, but is again and again the liberator. This is clear from the whole of the Old and New Testaments. Any other name that we give him is the name of an idol. Any other face that we give him distorts the Gospel into an ideology of alienation and oppression'.

The Christian basic movement and the later movement, 'Christians for Socialism', are not identical in the Netherlands, but since the conference in Lyons both have tended to read the Gospels together and to understand what liberation ought to mean in real life in Dutch society and who the poor really are. It is clear that much more attention will be given in the years ahead to a materialist exegesis of Scripture. The writings of such men as Huub Oosterhuis, the priest-poet, will inevitably influence the creation of a new theological language that will be increasingly used by groups and individuals outside the basic movement itself. Is this a good thing?

THE COMMISSION ON 'PLURIFORMITY'

So that the distinctive theology and Christian praxis of these basic groups should not become completely dissociated from the official Church and the theological institutions, Jan Ruijter, who was the pastor of the critical community at Ijmond and one of the original founders of the basic movement in the Netherlands, asked for a commission to be set up. In a conversation with the Bishop of Haarlem, he declared: 'A commission must be formed of experts drawn from different disciplines who will be given the task by the college of bishops to investigate whether there are any legitimate and possibly meaningful views and models of action of a social, political and theological or ecclesiastical kind within the groups and/or critical communities that are orientated towards renewal, views and models that may be of importance for the future of Church and society'. Jan Ruijter made this proposal in June 1972 and almost a year later, in May 1973, the conference of Dutch bishops agreed to it, so long as the conservative groups were included. In January 1974, the commission was introduced to the press and in May 1975 an interim report was presented. This consisted of two parts, as the commission had worked as two sub-commissions, one for the conservative groups and the other for the groups orientated towards renewal. Both parts of this report tried to do justice to the theological insights that were representative of each group. The report had this to say of the basic movement: 'We have ascertained that critical communities are very attractive to people who have become estranged from the Church. And we cannot too much stress that this new attraction is not gained or paid for by any sacrifice of Christian values. These communities attract more and more people because they accept Jesus and his mission'. In the same part of the report, the bishops were told:

'We have thought a great deal while we have been preparing this report about your task of protecting the unity of the Dutch province of the Church. We are firmly convinced that this unity is best served by maturity and diversity among believers. We regard it as fruitless simply to point to the serious differences in theology and Church order and then leave the problem at that. We think that even less is served by isolating and banishing formed communities. On the contrary, what we would like to see is many Christians from all kinds of Churches being inspired by what is good in the critical communities'.

The activities of the commission have not continued since the publication of this interim report. This is greatly to be regretted, because it cannot be denied that it is well worth while taking seriously into account the theology that is being practised on the periphery of the Church.

THE APPEAL OF 1977

At the end of 1977—the time at which I am writing—an appeal was made in the Netherlands to the basic movement. The working group entitled 'Service to Basic Groups and Critical Communities', which was formed in 1975 from Septuagint and other groups, hoped to group together the progressive Christian communities in the Netherlands. It is clear from this passage in the appeal how many different developments that have taken place in the recent past can be seen in a single context: 'The word basic group is used in the Netherlands as a collective name for Christians who have read both the Bible and the newspaper too closely to let themselves be held in the grip of a Church that is uncommitted and remote from the world, people who therefore have been forced to leave the Church or only just remained in it and have been trying together with two or three others to see whether things cannot be better outside. They do not think of themselves as people who know better. On the contrary, there is only one thing that they know with certainty—and this marks the essential beginning of their opposition—and that is that the Church begins with people and never the other way around. This insight has led them to form groups which, by thinking and doing, aim in different ways and at different levels to bring the Church back to man. . . . However different the points of departure and the ways of life of all these groups may be, they have all made the same discovery—that the Church should be there for people, that the best of our Jewish and Christian tradition is concerned with doing justice to insignificant people, with liberating the oppressed and the deprived here and in the Third World. . . . Inspired and encouraged by that Third World, our basic groups are characterized by their shared awareness of poverty and by the desire to obtain a good view and grasp of it. There are, after all, many forms of poverty and it is found a long way away and also deep in our own existence. There is illiteracy far beyond our own environment and poverty of language in our midst. There is the poverty of peasants, tea-pickers and seasonal labourers thousands of miles from us and the poverty of the unemployed, the overemployed and the isolated individuals in our midst. . . . We would like to reflect more deeply about these questions with groups and individuals in order to give more form and power to the world-wide movement of people at the basis and we would do this in the light of the ineradicable biblical vision of justice and peace'.

There are about a hundred or so known basic groups spread over the whole of the Netherlands and consisting of between thirty and five-hundred members belonging to the Catholic or the Reformed tradition or in some cases to no particular confession. In the Netherlands today, a renewed search is being made for clarity, certainty, order and justice and an attempt is being made to bring the experimental phase to an end. These groups are again trying to champion the cause of freedom, to resist ossification and to continue to be a platform for the poor and insignificant people, especially those in their own midst. They feel a strong link with similar groups outside the Netherlands, groups working in solidarity in other parts of Europe and basic groups in Latin America. They certainly know what is meant, for example, by the theology of liberation, black theology and feminist theology.

The members of these Dutch groups are also developing a theological identity. They recognize themselves, for example, in all the analyses and theories, both Christian and non-Christian, which take as their starting point man's psychological and social alienation, his misery and poverty, the contrasts between classes and the world-wide structures of injustice. They feel close to all thought and action that is directed towards liberating man and increasing solidarity. Within the Judaeo-Christian tradition, they feel strongly related to all the minorities, sects, saints and heretics in whose teaching—from the time of the Old Testament prophets, through Jesus of Nazareth and down to the present day—prevailing religious practices and ideologies have been criticized in the light of the demand for greater freedom, equality, brotherhood and community.

Certain monastic groups have, for this reason, joined the basic movement. These members of religious communities have been reflecting about the theology of the evangelical counsels, some of them for as long as ten years (there has, for example, been a group of Dominicans living in international solidarity, the so-called Lorscheid movement, in existence since 1968[1]), asking themselves in particular how the vows of poverty, obedience and chastity can be experienced in such a way that these can become models leading to a society in which men live in greater freedom and solidarity with each other. These monastics have formed new communities in some cases or community links on the fringe of the official orders and congregations. Some of these groups are more orientated towards political actions, others tend to practise mysticism. Many are inter-confessional or trans-confessional. They are very often places where new theories or practices emerge.

A very interesting experiment in the practice of theology is the movement that has been associated with the Catholic theological college of Utrecht since 1970—the 'agogical theological education' (ATO). This was evolved to correct the academic tendency of theology in the Netherlands and provides a theological education for people who have not previously followed a preparatory scientific course of study. 'The ATO course aims to educate workers who can make use of the Jewish and Christian traditions and understand them as interwoven into the existing social structures. The critical function of these traditions with regard to the society of the time is carefully investigated and analyzed. On the basis of this analysis, the *anawim* or "poor" of the Old Testament are seen as those who are oppressed and suffering from the injustice of the social structures of the time. If this Judaeo-Christian criticism of society is really concerned with the "poor", then, according to the ATO course at Utrecht, there is a need also to be concerned with a study of various social movements, including, for example, Marxism, that have been the basis of various organizations that have claimed to be on the side of the poor and the oppressed for a century and a half, as the Judaeo-Christian movement was on the side of the poor more than two millennia ago. The ATO course therefore follows the experience of many different Christian groups and their theology in various parts of the world'. (This is taken from the ATO prospectus.) We may conclude that the Christian basic movement recognizes itself explicitly in this description provided by the ATO course of the practice of theology and looks forward to an increasing exchange with the leaders of that course.

CONCLUSION

It is not easy to systematize or even have a conspectus of non-university theology in the Netherlands. (This is probably also the case in other countries.) It can be found in thousands of papers, leaflets and small books published by very divergent Christian groups. Christian Holland has, after all, to be divided into Christian groups now, rather than into Churches. The lines connecting all these different groups are often not at all clear. In this article, I have outlined a general development and said something about certain movements, being mainly concerned with a search for new subjects in theology. I have also tended to stress the thinking and action of the basic groups and critical communities in the Netherlands. If I have emphasized their thinking it is because I am more familiar with theology than with practical activity.

Looking back over the past two decades, I would draw the following conclusions. There are, broadly speaking, four main variants in Christian attitudes today, at least in the Netherlands. The first is that of the conservative Christians. They are disquieted and accuse the university theologians of Modernism and, in one case at least, in the diocese of Roermond (Bishop Gijssen), are hoping to set up their own seminary. The second variant is that of the charismatic Christians with their special form of theology. The third is that of the basic groups and critical communities, who feel themselves to be closely related to the group called Christians for Socialism and regard the Gospel as a power that can change society, both on a small scale and on a large scale. The fourth position is that of the centre; its members try to prevent polarization and to find a theological reconciliation for antitheses.

Theologians who teach at universities cannot ignore these positions in their practice of theology. This is why university and non-university theology is so difficult to separate. It is even possible to ask—certainly here in the Netherlands—whether the university is still the proper subject of theology. Johann Baptist Metz has asked this question: Is that subject the scholar, the university teacher, the preacher, the pastor, the mystic, the individual Christian? Or is it, Metz asks, the different groups and communities, the members of which are writing a mystical and political account of their lives in imitation of Christ?[2] All that I have attempted to do in this article is to initiate an answer to these questions with regard to my own country.

Translated by David Smith

Notes

1. M. Xhaufflaire has made a theological analysis of the Lorscheid movement in his 'Christianisme critique et vie religieuse', *Le Supplément*, 94 (1970), pp. 353-85.

2. J. B. Metz, *Followers of Christ* (London & New York, 1978).

I have also consulted various publications of the groups concerned for this article as well as reviews and accounts of the events within the Dutch province of the Catholic Church.

André Rousseau and Jean-Pierre Leconte

The Social Conditions of Theological Activity

THE TRANSFORMATION[1] of the pattern of life of French theologians is basically the result of the growing surfeit of research and teaching posts, following on a dwindling in the number of publics to be formed. In this article I intend to interpret the way in which this situation is dealt with and the impact it has on a 'displacement' of theology. To be specific, I shall take as my subject the ambition, as declared and carried into effect, to develop theological competence among laypeople.

THE STATE OF THE PROBLEM

I shall start from a definition of theology, ready-made but provisional, describing it as the act which accounts systematically for the coherence that exists between the social behaviour of a group of believers and the goals this group sets itself in the name of its beliefs. In this definition it will be convenient to introduce two parameters, the rôle of which is essential: on the one hand, the religious experience of the Christian group is related to other experiences; on the other hand, within the 'Christian' group no two people believe in the same way.

When one considers the believing group from the point of view of its *social behaviour,* one is not simply concerned with the ensemble of actions and behavioural patterns which form what sociologists call the 'consequential dimensions' of religious identity[2]; it is more precisely a question of drawing attention to the fact that the theologian cannot give an account of the 'faith' independently of the way it is mediated histor-

12

ically: that is to say, of the entire range of relationships, habits, behavioural patterns and language with which a social body is endowed, which it engenders and controls. What is more, the very idea of social behaviour implies a work of inclusion/exclusion realized by the group in order to speak and act out its identity, its differentness. This is to say that the way in which the believing group describes and interprets itself is coextensive with the way in which it projects itself and justifies its position. From there on, theology emerges as a constituent element of the social activity of believers; it is itself a social activity. Far from intervening after the event in the work carried out by the group at its frontiers, it is both its judge and a party to it. One could further define theology as the act and exercise of authority which permits the group thus to work on its identity. In fact it is not necessary to be a professional theologian in order to be a Christian; but when one is a Christian, whether one professes it oneself or it has to be said by others, this is not unrelated to present or past activity of theologians. In return, because it is systematic discourse on belief, theology presupposes belief in its own discourse: a minimum of integration into the body of believers.

Examination of the discourse of theologians on the human sciences would doubtless offer a means for showing that it is the theologian who is displaced, even when he says he wants to displace himself. Indeed, from the moment when scientific modes of thought spread themselves in the intellectual field, the theologian must bring into play his own universal forms of understanding (philosophy); if he wants to preserve his capacity for initiative he must change his intellectual allegiances. In manifesting, sometimes ostentatiously, that he is giving up his old patterns of thought, he can give the impression that he is displaced. But if he needs to invent other ground rules for theological discourse, in order to preserve his social influence—in particular on clerics, to whom it is more especially directed—it is precisely because he cannot ignore the minimum required for his own integration into the group.

It is therefore impossible to treat of theological activity and even less of the transformation of theology, without taking as object of the analysis the *work of theologians,* or more exactly the effect of the work of theologians. Briefly, if theology says it is displaced, the sociologist asks himself how theologians have brought about this displacement.

Let me begin by distinguishing in the social activity of the theologian technical competence and social influence. The first is defined by a title, the fruit of negotiations between authorities competent to define and bestow that title; social influence is defined by a position, a function, which results from negotiations with authorities wielding analogous or different influence, virtually concurrent in any case.

Whether one takes it from the point of view of technical competence or social influence, the practice of the theologian is a subject for negotiation. To emphasise this is to give the 'displacement' of theology an objective content. It is not something that happens to a theologian in the way that sickness settles in an organism; nor is it a deliberate initiative. It consists of the effect of previous activity; it is a way of handling a range of activities and objective relations.

The two aspects that I began by distinguishing are dialectically linked. Competence is always affected to some extent by the social influence and is nothing without the position in which it can be exercised, which gives it its authority. The suggested distinction has the merit of drawing attention to two systems of relations which determine theological practice: one defines the competence, the other the authority. To ask about the relative autonomy of these two systems of relations is already, perhaps, to pose correctly the question of 'displacement' or transformation: is not the present situation characterized by the fact that competence depends more strictly than in the past on institutions that simultaneously confer authority and power? The crisis in these institutions reflects back on the definition of competence itself and having deported the theologian, displaces theology.

Before making a more detailed diagnosis, I should stress the fact that to put the displacement of theology into a sociological perspective does not consist simply in seeing how the theologian reacts in the search for theological models in which to define his rôle. Above all, it is necessary to show how the prospect of new discourses and new rôles implies a search for and negotiation of social effects, not only as regards the recipients, but also as regards peers, rivals and those who occupy positions where religious legitimacy is determined. What is more, all other things being equal, the sociologist employed by religious organizations or militants in a political movement, would find himself in the same situation: obliged to control the effects of his sociological practice, but at the same time called upon by his counterparts, who hold the monopoly of 'scientific' sociology, to give proof of the scientific and therefore *bona fide* character of the sociology he practices.

The 'displacement' of theology consists in a transaction imposed by the state of the theological market and variations of religious interest. It is a question of a new formulation of theological interest.

Talk of *theological interest* will only appear to be begging the question to champions of the disinterestedness of theologians. On the other hand, the concept is a compelling one if one is seeking to answer the question: what is it that gives importance to the things of which theologians speak, to the problem areas in which they are trying to become specialists? In response to this question it is not enough to maintain that the most legitimate theologians (attached to universities or experts among the church authorities) put forward as important the problems about which they are concerned. It would be equally simplistic or partial to say that the grass-roots, the public or whatever, force on theologians the object of their inquiry. It is necessary to show how the particular interest of theologians is mediated through the positions they occupy in a particular field and among a body of professionals. It is this field which, as focus of a competition for power, imposes on each theologian, in virtue of the position he occupies, problems and methods that are both technical and strategic.

This implies that the process of structural development proper to the corpus of theologians, together with the positions of legitimacy, the ways of achieving it and the strategies that result from it should be brought into the open (and related to one another). In this perspective the 'displacement' of theology could well be no more than the reorganization of the rules of access to theological competence and the correlative social influence: the term reorganization is not, one should recall, to be understood as decision, but as the structural effect of transformations in the religious field, as modification of the common-places that ensure communication. Without overdoing the paradox, one could speak of reorganization without a plan for reorganization, and it would be interesting to compare Vatican effects to elaborate a *ratio studiorum* with the more or less spontaneous adjustments I am going to analyze here.

A SIGN OF THE TIMES: THE AMBITION TO GIVE LAY-PEOPLE A THEOLOGICAL FORMATION

For some years now numerous organizations have been emerging in France offering to lay-people—in a variety of forms: meetings, courses of formation, correspondence courses—the possibility of acquiring theological competence. I shall not undertake here a systematic description of these programmes. On the basis of a number of documents, I shall show how this phenomenon illustrates the conquest by theologians of a new area of competence and the negotiation of new social influence. I shall try to understand how theologians, no longer finding among the clergy a satisfactory or sufficiently rewarding social base, are developing a new strategy of reconquest.

A *strategy for reconversion*

Many of the institutions which offer a theological formation to lay-people are converted major seminaries whose professors have thus been able to renegotiate their status by justifying their existence through a forward-looking vision of the functions of theology. This reconversion often takes the form of a profanatory or magical action, if by that one understands a diversion of legitimacy or, better, an attempt to transfer a mode of exercising cultural power from the clerical field to a field alien to the former activity. This latter fact can help one to understand some of the characteristics and contradictions of these enterprises.

Thus the man in charge of one of these adapted institutions has said: 'We thought that the reorganization of seminaries did not have a future as a solution for theological reflection in the Church. In a Church which wants to reflect a little on what goes on in the world as well as within herself, theological reflection cannot be the preserve of a particular, in this case clerical, elite . . .'[3] This twofold ambition: to put theology in tune with culture and to modify the distribution of power in the Church, must be related to the circumstances in which it appeared. It all turns out, in fact, as if theology, in a state of crisis as far as recruitment and its public are concerned, was going to seek outside itself the way of conducting a discourse adapted to modern culture and those to whom that discourse is directed, who at other times have been reduced to a state of passivity and subordination.

Finally, the expressed wish to destroy the monopoly of the 'clerical élite' refers to the competition of their ideologies: professional theologians see to it that they share power in order not to lose it entirely, and in so doing challenge the earlier forms of their social power.[4]

This renegotiation of the theologian's rôle is not only the business of seminary professors, holders of theological titles, previously restricted to a reduced geographical and social area; one also finds professors in faculties of theology who create correspondence courses or parallel formation. There is no need to emphasize the fact that the effect of these practices is to widen the theologian's sphere of influence and therefore to restructure the relationship between competence and power, between theology-producing institutions and the social field; between theologians and the religious authority. That is why a sociological analysis of these practices will concentrate not on the content of the formation but on the social relationships which define it and which it, in its turn, modifies.

It is not so much theology that is being displaced as it is the theologian who is trying to renegotiate his status. He defines himself through his cultural rôle, his capacity to treat areas of knowledge whose origin is outside his own sphere of competence ('the world') to which he is beginning, on occasion, to give way.

This renegotiation is concerned also with a de jure or de facto recognition of a new function which sets itself up as a task for the future:

access to theological competence and through that, it is claimed, to the ideological power of the laity.[5]

This strategy implies a competition with the religious powers whose want of insight and even incompetence will come in for criticism.[6]

The third major implication of this strategy of reconversion is that the pedagogical approach will change. Teaching lay people forces one to get closer to a 'normal' way of exercising intellectual authority: group work and so on; spreading the news that one is doing the new theology and marketing the clients (competition with similar systems and the programmes of Catholic Action, which has acquired its own forms of expertise and its own power strategy in the Church). Here already is a phenomenon to which we shall return later: the theologian is led to 'think' his interventions and their content in a different way and this reconversion will be more or less profound according as the group of lay people insists more or less on its own mode of relating.

Social conditions making this reconversion possible

The various factors related to the constitution of publics and institutions[7] reveal four basic characteristics. Predominantly female adult publics; professions orientated towards social action, cultural diffusion and the reorganization of collective life in general; populations strongly integrated with the Church, and frequently occupying or aspiring to posts of responsibility within it; finally publics strongly motivated towards 'high-level' religious formation, whose cultural aspirations, far from threatening their availability for theological formation, reinforce it.

These four traits can be reduced to one, which sums them all up: cultural dependence or, which comes to the same thing, preparedness to pay the symbolic price for 'initiation' into the mastery of goods, in the efficacity of which they believe. Only very rarely do institutions offer positions of authority to initiated lay-people[8] and this paradox merits analysis. It even happens, in fact, that certain lay-people, whose competence is recognised, refuse the institutional posts offered them, preferring to take less 'remarkable' posts: for example, someone who had received a diploma at an institute for catechesis refused a post as parish catechist, took other salaried work and agreed, in a voluntary capacity, to accompany other catechists in their work as 'trainers of trainers'. This case seems to us typical in the sense that it is representative of the ground on which theologians in the process of reconversion can develop their initiative by cultivating a double misunderstanding. The case described just now in fact reproduces fairly accurately the strategy of theologians who specialize in the formation of this sort of competence. On the one hand theological competence is ostantatiously disassociated from any kind of 'professional' characteristic, a distinction which distinguishes them from university-based theologians who for their part claim that the most legitimate way of practising theology is to have professional status.[9] On the other hand, this denial of the status of the theologian as a professional is in fact a device, a way of achieving social influence by negotiating indirectly for the status of 'trainer of trainers', which is less prominent institutionally-speaking and less identifiable with clerical status.

The stratagems for emancipation develop successfully, therefore, when on the one hand, clerics formerly engaged in subordinate theological tasks (formation of *prêtres de base* or catechists) and, on the other, lay-people more or less closely connected with catechesis or the liturgical renewal, whose scholarly and religious bent disposes them to receive messages proposing 'enlightenment', 'deepening', 'renewal' and 'new understanding', meet and understand one another.[10]

When lay-people 'in training' wish to talk about their discoveries, they send back to their trainers the perfect echo of the need which the latter have themselves produced and cultivated: they express satisfaction at having been initiated into a culture of which they were ignorant, and at being in a position to master new social representations of their beliefs and of themselves.

Everything continues, therefore, as though the parties involved had an interest in cultivating the ambiguity of their relationship. The trainers wish to train, but not so much for tasks as for non-institutionizable forms of competence, conformable to the image they have of their own rôle. Lay-people, on their side, will frequently regard their trainers as convincing and convinced preachers. But one could argue that ambiguity is an integral part of the market: how, in effect, is one to maintain a 'demand' for formation without negotiable objectives except by giving prominence to motives and leaving technical competence vague? How is one to get people to believe in the objectives and content of formation, except by invoking culturally recognized expertise (the human sciences) and playing the card of modernity ('to affront the cultural mutations of our time')?[11]

CONCLUSIONS: THEOLOGIANS IN THE SOCIAL FIELD

The example of the strategies brought into play by theologians in order to 'form' lay-people throws light for us on the way in which the social context determines the place and the practice of those who possess theological qualifications but no post. In choosing this example I ran the risk of reducing the relationship of the theological field to the social field to one of relations with clients. In contrast to the usual picture theologians present of their activity, I wanted to recall that there is no face-to-face confrontation, theologians versus laity, and that the picture of a 'supply-and-demand' relationship is false, since it is still necessary to account for each of the terms. In fact, the formation offered is addressed in the first instance to lay people interested in such formation. One has to see how theologians come to the point of thinking up this particular solution to their employment problems. I have shown that this choice is in large measure determined by the affinities that exist between the position of theologians and that of lay-people, both of them having an interest in cultivating a certain degree of uncertainty about their objective relationship. If lay-people find in theological formation reassurance for their religious affiliation, clerics find in it, *ipso facto*, the means for creating a need for theology and for renegotiating both their competence and their social influence. But this renegotiation is not going on with lay people alone; occupying the field left free by the scholar theologians, theologians formerly engaged in the formation of clerics are renegotiating the areas and institutions in which theological legitimacy is defined.

Translated by Sarah Fawcett

Notes

1. This text is part of a research project concerned with a sociological treatment of the idea of a 'displacement or transformation of theology'. The field chosen for observation was the Rhône-Alpes region of France.

2. Ch. Y. Glock, 'Y a-t-il un réveil religieux aux Etats-Unis?', in *Archives de Sociologie des Religions*, 12 (1961), p. 36.

3. One of those in charge of the Centre Théologique de Meylan (Grenoble): reported by C. Marechal, 'Formation des adultes chrétiens', in *Vivante Eglise*, (January 1975), p. 26.

4. 'In the beginning, the theologian had the lion's share . . . as a result not so much of the number or volume of his contributions as of the moment in time: he intervened last, as if theology was the universal science recapitulating and subsuming all the other branches of knowledge. With time the situation has changed a great deal. In the first place, the interventions of experts have much less authority than they did in the past; working parties and round tables carry quite as much weight. The experts are no longer the specialist "fathers" of other disciplines: physics, medicine, sociology, history . . . Finally, the theological contributions are more often than not thought up during the

session, and not drawn up in advance.' C. Marechal, 'Formation', p. 28.

5. 'Theologians have difficulty in moving beyond the confines of their own discipline. No one has succeeded in coordinating formation for want of reflection as much on the future of the Church as on the type of formation that will prepare that future and bring it about . . . One should not be content to reproduce the models of formation produced by the seminaries. Formation must enter into a critical age. It must take account of the present situation in which the Church finds itself and give evidence of clear sightedness about the future, since one senses already that new forms of organization for the Church are on the way'. One of those in charge at the Institut d'Etudes Pastorales at Religieuses (Lyons). Quoted by C. Marechal, 'Formation' Part 3, *Vivante Église* (March 1975), p. 91.

6. 'Centres like this one, or others, will play an absolutely decisive rôle in the Church of tomorrow, comparable, *mutatis mutandis,* to the rôle of the monasteries in the Middle Ages. If, as one is able to foresee, the strongest and most authentic communities, breaking increasingly with the party line, tomorrow constitute the essential of the ecclesial system, they will feel the need of an organic link with the more structured milieus, which will serve them as a point of reference, spiritual as well as theological'. One of those in charge of the Centre Saint Dominique, l'Arbresle. Quoted by C. Marechal, op cit., p. 93.

'I feel more and more that the formation centres are going to become the nerve centres of the Church's life, if only for the very simple reason that they are the only places capable of forming competent ministers. For in every field competence is proving itself to be indispensable'. One of those in charge of the Institut d'Etudes Pastorales et Religieuses (Lyons), C. Marechal, op. cit.

7. This refers to the Centre Théologique de Meylan, the Centre Lyonnais d'Etudes Religieuses at Pastorales, an organization in Saint-Etienne, and the Centre Saint Dominique at l'Arbresle; to these should be added the course in theological formation for lay-people at the Institut Catholique in Paris.

8. 'The Church today has need of lay theologians . . . Other establishments than the Institut Catholique in Paris have undertaken this task . . . It remains to us to search together for the best form of ecclesial service that newly-qualified lay-theologians will soon be able to undertake'. Cardinal Marty, 'Communication aux théologiens réunis à l'occasion de leur assemblée de "concertation des facultés de théologie" ' (24 August 1977).

9. 'This theology, indispensable for the life of the believing Church, will not emerge at the "grass-roots", in communities without theologians, in the professional sense of the term. In order to maintain the level of theological activity and theological production throughout the Church, we need at least a few great theologians in each century, as well as theological institutions'. Père Liège, director of Unité d'Enseignement at de Recherche de Théologie et de Sciences Religieuses at the Institut Catholique in Paris, at a round-table on the theme 'Can theology be taught?', *Informations Catholiques Internationales,* No. 502 (15 May 1976), p. 46.

10. The case of women religious, who constitute an important part of the clientele, far from representing a different situation from that of the recruitment of lay-people, accentuates the characteristics (in particular readiness to believe in the efficacity of theology) that I have described.

11. Which results in the formation of lay-people ready to listen to the 'new' theological discourse much more than formerly. The interviews with lay-people following courses in theological formation carried out by de Chalendar, are eloquent on this point. Cf., *Rapport sur al Formation Théologique des Laics*, drawn up at the request of the Archdiocese of Paris (1975).

Elisabeth Schüssler Fiorenza

Towards a Liberating and Liberated Theology: Women Theologians and Feminist Theology in the USA

WHEN IN 1847 Antoinette Brown decided to study theology and to take a theological degree from Oberlin she met with considerable resistance from her parents, friends, and advisers. Nevertheless she persisted in her goal. After considerable debate, the faculty at Oberlin decided that they could not deny her the privilege of applying herself to religious studies. However, after Antoinette Brown completed her program of theological studies in 1850 she and another female student were not allowed to graduate. Only in 1878 did Oberlin grant her an honorary MA and in 1908 an honorary doctor of divinity degree. In 1853 she was the first woman ordained in the USA, but consistent with her growing religious liberalism she resigned from her pastorate a year later. Nevertheless she inspired other women to pursue theological studies and to enter the ministry.[1]

WOMEN SEMINARIANS AND THEOLOGIANS

Today the number of female students in theological schools and seminaries steadily increases. In prestigious Protestant seminaries women constitute up to fifty per cent of the student body. Women's groups within the theological schools have pressured faculty and administration to take women's problems and questions more seriously. Most major theological schools therefore offer women's studies seminars and support women's centres. Yet most institutions not only have very few women faculty members, but their faculties are seldom aware of their covert or overt sexism and have almost no academic training in women's studies in religion. Therefore the need is felt to create the institutional space necessary for women to shape their own theological education and to explore alternative ways of practising the ministry and theology. One most successful attempt, the Seminary Quarter at Grailville[2] initiated by Church Women United and by the Grail movement, attracts students from all theological schools during the summer months. Yet, despite well-meaning attempts to integrate women into theological seminaries and to develop their perspective in theological education, the situation of a woman graduating from a seminary is not so different from that of Antoinette Brown. True, a woman graduate receives, like her male colleagues a theological degree; but only about one-third of the clergy-women are able to move into ministerial positions immediately upon the completion of their seminary training.[3] Most of them find themselves in subordinate positions, especially in educational work with women and children; only very rarely is a woman hired for an independent pastorate or pulpit. The increase in the number of students in seminaries and theological schools does therefore not indicate a greater influence of women in the professional ministry. Since theological schools often do not attract enough qualified male applicants and struggle for their financial survival, the greater number of highly qualified women admitted to the schools in view of economical pressures does not imply an actual increase of women's presence in the professional ministry.

Whereas the biographical dictionary of *Notable American Women 1607–1950* lists many names of ministers, evangelists, missionaries, religious educators, founders and leaders, it does not have the category of 'theologian', even though it acknowledges women historians, psychologists, classical and literary scholars, and archaeologists. The history of women in the academic profession of theology and women's contributions to religious studies still needs to be written. Today about two to four hundred women qualify as professional theologians in the USA in so far as they have a doctorate in theology or religious studies or are near its completion.[4] Women teach religious studies and theology in colleges, universities and theological schools. The majority of the women faculty are, however, either in less prestigious colleges and schools with heavy teaching loads and little emphasis on research, or they are found at the junior non-tenured level as instructors or assistant professors. A growing number of women with doctoral degrees are not able to obtain a teaching position at all. Because of explicit or implicit 'nepotism' rules, married women especially are often not hired for full-time positions. They are relegated to underpaid adjunct positions or are forced to take jobs in inferior institutions. Wife-husband teams are especially vulnerable, since patriarchal administrators still take it for granted that the wife will move and give up her career if the husband is denied tenure or a renewal of contract.

In spite of the rhetoric of ecclesiastics in defence of the Christian family, theological institutions do not hesitate to destroy marriages and families in order to preserve the patriarchal and clerical academic system that has no room for married persons who are scholars in their own right.[5] The dedication in books to wives or female collaborators indicates the extent to which male academic careers are supported by women who not only perform auxiliary services as housekeeping or typing but research or actually compose the book. The widely-published relationship between Karl Barth and Charlotte von Kirschbaum is paradigmatic of this practice.

Very few women hold senior-level, permanent tenured faculty positions and are free to develop their own theological interests and style. Likewise women seldom make it to the higher administrative ranks of theological institutions and at present only one is the head of a theological school. Because of the political pressures of the academic women's movement and governmental affirmative action plans in general, and because of the work of the Women's Caucus-Religious Studies[6] in particular, a few women have been appointed in the past five years to the governing boards of major theological professional societies, to the editorial boards of leading theological journals, and two women have served as presidents of theological societies. The impact of these women on policy issues and the real power structures within the professional societies was, however, negligible, since they were not able to break through the network of the 'old boys' club'. They served the purposes of token liberalism more than they served actually to influence the power structures and ideologies of the theological profession. Because of the dismal prospects of the job-market the impact of women on the theological profession will probably even more decline and not improve in the foreseeable future. The little progress that has been made in past years is in danger of being obliterated.

Not much has changed in the last hundred and more years since Antoinette Brown entered the theological field. Only grudgingly admitted to a clerical, male profession, women students as well as faculty remain marginal to the theological enterprise. They are at best tolerated by their male colleagues and by academic administrators and at worst they are permanently turned away from theological studies and research altogether. In any case, they do not have any substantial impact on the way in which theology is done. The professional theologian remains in the public consciousness 'he'. This marginality of women in the theological profession is, however, not merely typical of the North American situation, but of other countries. On my last visit to Germany, I asked a university professor if a woman occupied a chair at a traditional Protestant or Catholic theological faculty. He assured me that at Catholic faculties laymen can now be 'habilitated' and become professors. When I stressed that I was interested in knowing whether a woman theologian was a member of an established faculty he turned to his housekeeper and asked sarcastically: 'Do you want to become my successor?' Apparently, for him, the housekeeper was in the same position *vis-à-vis* academic theology as qualified women theologians. What matters is not qualifications and publications but the fact that we are women.

THE FEMINIST ANALYSIS OF THE ACADEMIC
INSTITUTIONS OF THEOLOGY

This incident made it, however, clear to me that the situation of women theologians in America *is* different from that of their European sisters. An American colleague might have had the same sentiments but he would have never voiced them with such candour. Because of the women's movement in the USA 'androcentrism', or sexism and discrimination against women, is exposed more and more as structural evil and personal fault. Liberal professors of theology would no more risk the accusation of sexism than that of racism. They are aware that American women are no longer grateful to be tolerated on the fringes of the professions but that they seek full participation in them.

Feminist analyses of culture and religion have moreover shown that full participation of women in academic life and research will only be possible when the patriarchal and sexist structures of academic institutions are changed. Women do not just demand to be tolerated by the academy and to be integrated into the clockwork of male careers. By organizing professional women and by initiating legislation and affirmative action plans, feminists seek to change the patriarchal systems of the academy as well as the patriarchal-sexist attitudes of male academicians and students so that women are able fully to participate in intellectual work and academic research. Yet at the same time feminists realize that it does not suffice simply to incorporate more women into the academic system. What is necessary is to overcome the sex-typing of the academic professions in general and of academic theology specifically.

Although numerous critical analyses of church and clerical structures exist, critical evaluations of the theological profession as such are scarce. Most recently liberation theologians[7] have pointed out that theology in an European and North American context is white and middle-class and as such shares in the cultural imperialism of Europe and the USA. Theology as the domain of white clergy reflects the interests of the white middle-class community. Since theologians, theological schools, and publishing houses depend on grants and money from the rich, they have to cater for the interests of the white establishment.

Feminist theologians claim that this analysis of the life-setting of the theological discipline does not probe far enough. Christian academic theology is not only white, middle-class and establishment but white, middle-class and *male,* and shares in the sex-typing of academic institutions and the professions. The androcentric character of the discipline is as pervasive and personally threatening as the race and class issues. Theology can only become *humanized* and liberated from oppressive sex-stereotypes when males take seriously the challenges of the feminist critique and begin to analyze their own privileges and practice as men in a male-typed profession.

The institutions of the theological discipline share the androcentric character of other academic institutions.[8] The public image of the theological profession is sex-typed and recruitment to the profession generally has functioned to exclude or to discourage women from seeking admission to the academic or ministerial ranks of the discipline. Moreover, interactions—especially in the top echelons of the profession—are exclusive and informal, based on unstated norms and implying a social, male solidarity within an exclusive, club-like, and often clerical environment. Not so much qualifications but the prestige of the school and sponsor-protégé relationships determine access to financial resources, and to the inner circles and power centers of the discipline. The *Doktorvater* system treats male students as potential professors and successors with preference in so far it makes scholarships available to them, provides important connections with established colleagues in the field, and fills influential senior positions by informal recommendations. Aware of the male orientation of the theological profession, professors are not inclined to sponsor and to support the career of female students with the same enthusiasm. They implicitly recognize that women will not be able to establish themselves as scholarly authorities in the field and therefore will not expand the power and increase the academic standing of the *Doktorvater* or continue his scholarship as his successors after his retirement. Male students on the other hand do not gain the same means of advancement by working with a woman professor since she is not a fully accepted member of the informal, professorial 'male club'. Women theologians are thus not able to penetrate the professional networks and to succeed in a male-typed theological profession.

Furthermore, the judgment of whether a theologian is of 'top' rank usually depends on his or her affiliation with prestigious institutions, and association with the leading men in the field, and on the publicity received in reviews or discussions of publications and research. On all three counts women theologians are likely to be disadvantaged. They usually do not have senior positions in prestigious theological schools, they are not promoted by senior men to the same degree as their male colleagues, and their research and publications receive relatively little attention from men or women, since men are the supposed authorities in the field. Moreover, women students are often channelled through doctoral dissertations into the fringe areas of theology. In my opinion it is no accident that in NT studies for instance women are over-represented in Gnostic studies or in research into the Apocalypse, a NT book widely neglected by serious exegetes.

Finally, because women do not 'fit' into a male-typed theological discipline, their presence in professional networks and departmental committees causes considerable rôle-confusion. Men, students as well as professors, do not know how to relate to women as academicians but fall back on the traditional norms governing male-female relationships. Women are treated like perpetual daughters dependent on the fatherly authority of their teachers, as secretaries or research assistants, as caring mother-figures, as aggressive 'bitches', or as erotic objects for flirtation. Men rarely know how to relate to women as interesting colleagues and as theological authorities in their own right. A letter of a young woman theologian high-lights this point. She reports that expressing interest in the work of established, senior colleagues often leads to dinner-invitations and to sexual advances. 'Like her male counterparts, she needs colleagues to confirm the validity and importance of her ideas. But she finds herself in a position where she never can know whether a colleague was interested in her ideas or in her body'.[9]

FEMINIST THEOLOGY AND THE LIBERATION OF THEOLOGY

The presupposition and consequence of the full participation of women in the academic study of theology would be the transformation not only of theological institutions and male theologians but of theology as a discipline, of its contents and methods. Feminist theologians argue for the full inclusion of women in the theological profession not just because of career advancement in a male-typed institution but because they are convinced that theological and ecclesial structures have to be liberated from all forms of racism, classism, and sexism, if they are to serve people and not to contribute to their oppression. Sexism in theology is not so much just a personal fault as a structural evil that distorts and corrupts theology and the Christian message.

In so far as feminist theology concerns itself with the theological analysis of the myths, mechanisms, systems, and institutions which keep women oppressed, it shares in the objectives and expands the analysis of critical theology. As against the so-called objectivity and neutrality of academic theology, feminist theologians assert that theology always serves definite interests and therefore has critically to evaluate its own institutional basis and its primary allegiance. Theology has to abandon its so-called neutrality and has to take the part of the oppressed.

By positively expressing the new human possibilities of women and men, by creating and promoting new symbols, myths, and life-styles, by raising new questions and different horizons, feminist theology shares in the concerns and goals of liberation theology. But because women belong to all races, classes, and cultures and were throughout centuries oppressed by patriarchy, its scope is more universal and radical than that of critical and liberation theology. Since the beginnings and subsequent history of Christian theology were immersed in cultural and ecclesial patriarchy, women whether white or black, rich or poor, married or not, never could take a significant rather than marginal part of the formulation of Christian faith and theology. The writers of the OT lived in Palestine, Augustine in North Africa, and Thomas in Europe. Yet their theology is no less formulated from a male perspective than that of Barth, Niebuhr or Teilhard de Chardin. Because theology has been and is rooted in male experience,[10] traditional theology has ignored the experience and contributions of women.

Those feminist theologians[11] who have experienced Christian faith and tradition as liberating from cultural sexism attempt to rediscover and to spell out those liberating elements within Christian faith and theology. They insist that for too long the Christian traditions were recorded and studied by theologians who consciously or not interpreted them from the patriarchal perspective of male dominance. For instance, it is apparent from Paul's letters that women were missionaries and leaders in the early Church before Paul and co-equal with Paul. Yet androcentric reconstructions of early Christianity assume that women were marginal to the early Christian missionary movement and therefore reduce women's contributions to that of 'helping out' Paul. However, if women are to get in touch with their own roots, historical interpretations must cease to project back into the first century the marginality of women in our own Church and culture. A feminist hermeneutics has to point out the centrality of women in the early Christian movement,[12] if the claim that Christianity is from its very beginnings inherently sexist should be proven unfounded.

Yet a hermeneutical revision of Christian theology and interpretation is only a partial solution to the problem, since it is apparent that the Christian past and present and not just its theological interpretations and records have victimized women.[13] It does not suffice merely to correctly understand the Christian tradition and its symbolic frameworks. Any understanding of Christian theology as 'the actualizing continuation of the Christian history of interpretation'[14] overlooks how the tradition is a source not only of truth and liberation but of repression and domination. Therefore theology must critically evaluate and reject those traditions that have contributed to the oppression of women. As Christian theology has rejected the traditions of anti-Judaism, even when found in the Bible, so it has now to reject all sexist traditions even if they are rooted in biblical texts. Christian theology has to spell out and to affirm that revelation and truth are found only in those traditions and texts that transcend and criticize patriarchal culture and androcentric religion.[15] Only those traditions that express the word of God in *human* and not in sexist language can be liberating for women and men.

The critique of androcentric language is therefore central to the feminist reconstruction of Christian faith and theology. Since language is not just a vehicle of communication but determines our perception of ourselves and of reality, androcentric God-language and symbolism do not engender a religious self-understanding of women or of a reality inclusive of women. On the contrary, these impede women's ego-development[16] and legitimize feminine cultural stereotypes and the ecclesial subordination of women. Even though Christian theology has always known that God transcends gender as well as race, its speaking of God as Father and as Son communicates to women and men the fact that maleness and not femaleness expresses and encompasses the divine reality. The recent Vatican statement against the ordination of women documents the negative consequences of androcentric God-language for the role of women in the Church. The document's insistence on the maleness of Christ and on the masculine rather than human character of salvation serves, however, not so much as an argument against the ordination of women but demonstrates that the central mysteries of Christian faith are male and exclusive of women. As long as the central Christian symbols of faith are expressed in male language and imagery, women have to insist that the language and symbolism of God are one-sided and need to be balanced by female imagery and symbolism rooted in women's experience. We must learn to speak of God as Father and Mother, as Son and Daughter, as she and he. Until female God-language is commonly accepted in Christian theology and worship[17] women will not be able to recognize themselves in the image and likeness of God.

In conclusion: Feminist theologians are well aware that their vision of a non-sexist, non-oppressive God cannot be embodied in 'old wineskins' but has to be expressed in new theological structures and language. If change is to occur, a circular movement is necessary.[18] Efforts concentrated on bringing women's experience to bear on theology will not succeed unless theological institutions are changed to accept the presence and expertise of women as well as to allow feminist theologizing. On the other hand, efforts to change established theological institutions cannot be far-reaching enough if theological language, myth, and symbols serve to maintain women's marginal status and secondary role in theology and Church. Structural change in theology and the evolution of a feminist theology have to go hand in hand.

Feminist theologians therefore seek to ground their theologizing in the practice of 'consciousness-raising' and 'sisterhood'. Consciousness-raising makes us aware of our own oppression by sexism and our oppression of others. It helps to overcome the fears and emotional reactions engendered by the challenge of feminist theology to the basic symbolism and tenets of traditional theology. Expressed in biblical language, consciousness-raising engenders conversion and a new vision, names the realities of sin and grace, and leads to a community of emancipatory solidarity.

Sisterhood provides such a community of emancipatory solidarity for those who acknowledge their oppression by religious and cultural sexism and are on the way to liberation. Feminist theologians in the USA have begun to build structures of 'sisterhood' which support women in the male-typed discipline of academic theology or pastoral ministry and provide the basis for a new way of doing theology. These structures of bonding are ecumenical and interdisciplinary in the best sense of the words. This article is also written to initiate international contacts among women theologians and to foster feminist theological dialogue on an international level. Only when women theologians from different countries come together to create new theological structures and to engender the liberation and transformation of theology will we be able to bring about radical change in the practice and theory of theology.

Notes

1. B. M. Solomon, 'Blackwell, Antoinette Louisa Brown', in *Notable American Women 1607-1950, I* (Cambridge, Mass., 1968), pp. 158-61.

2. Cf. the report issued each summer from Grailville, Ohio. The Seminary Quarter is a six-week programme. It attempts to explore not only new forms of theology but new ways of learning. Facilitators make possible a living-learning community; a resource faculty assists students in exploring their individual theological projects and helps in the preparation of group-projects. Topics explored are: liberation theology and a feminist critique; language, myth, and symbol; sexuality and spirituality; curriculum for Christian feminism; self as source for theologizing; assumptions about institutional and social change; biography as theology, exploring ministry, or wholeness and worship.

3. E. Wilbur Bock, 'The Female Clergy: A Case of Professional Marginality', in A. Theodore (ed.), *The Professional Woman* (Cambridge, Mass., 1971), pp. 599-611; A. R. Jones, 'Differential Recruitment of Female Professionals: A Case Study of Clergy Women', ibid., pp. 355-65.

4. It is difficult to obtain exact statistics. The Registry of the Women's Caucus-Religious Studies lists about 230 names. Yet this list is far from being complete.

5. Cf. A. Russel Hochschild, 'Inside the Clockwork of Male Careers', in F. Howe (ed.), *Women and the Power to Change,* The Carnegie Commission on Higher Education (1975), pp. 47-80.

6. The Women's Caucus-Religious Studies was initiated at the national annual AAR/SBL convention in Atlanta in 1971. It publishes a registry of women theologians to facilitate the placement of women graduate students and faculty and a quarterly newsletter to provide a public forum for women in the profession. It also sponsors working sessions on women in religion at the annual conventions to facilitate public discussion on feminist theological issues. The best papers of these sessions are published.

7. Cf. e.g., F. Herzog, 'Liberation Theology Begins at Home', *Christianity and Crisis* (13 May, 1974) and 'Liberation Hermeneutics as Ideology Critique', *Interpretation* 28 (1974), pp. 387-403.

8. C. F. Epstein, 'Encountering the Male Establishment: Sex-Status Limits on Women Careers in the Professions', in A. Theodore, op. cit., pp. 39-51; P. A. Graham, 'Women in Academe', ibid., pp. 720-40; A. Rich, 'Toward a Woman-Centered University', in F. Howe, op. cit., pp. 15-46.

9. *Women's Caucus-Religious Studies Newsletter* 2 (1974), p. 5.

10. For the analysis of the theological understanding of sin rooted in male experience, cf. Valerie Saiving Goldstein, 'The Human Situation: A Feminine View', in *The Journal of Religion* 40 (1960), pp. 100-12; J. Plaskow, *Sex, Sin and Grace: Women's Experience and the Theologies of Reinhold Niebuhr and Paul Tillich* (unpubl. dissertation, Yale, 1975).

11. For a discussion of the goals and literature of feminist theology, see my article 'Feminist Theology as a Critical Theology of Liberation', in *Theological Studies* 36 (1975), pp. 605-26; J. Plaskow, 'The Feminist Transformation of Theology', (unpubl. paper); and C. P. Christ, 'The New Feminist Theology: A Review of the Literature', *Religious Studies Review* (forthcoming).

12. Cf. my articles, 'The Rôle of Women in the Early Christian Movement', *Concilium* 7 (January 1976) (not in English); 'The Study of Women in Early Christianity. Some Methodological Considerations', in *Proceedings of the College Theology Society 1977* (forthcoming), and 'Spirit, Word and Power. Women in early Christian Groups', in McLaughlin & R. Reuther, *Women of the Spirit* (forthcoming).

13. Cf. the contention of M. Daly that Christian faith and symbols are inherently sexist, M. Daly, *Beyond God the Father: Toward a Philosophy of Women's Liberation* (Boston, 1973).

14. Cf. E. Schillebeeckx, *The Understanding of Faith* (New York, 1974).

15. Cf. my article, 'Interpreting Patriarchal Traditions', in L. Russel (ed.), *The Liberating Word. A Guide to Nonsexist Interpretations of the Bible* (Philadelphia, 1976), pp. 39-61.

16. Cf. N. R. Goldenberg, 'Freud, the Fathers and the Jewish Christian Traditions', in *Psychocultural Review* (forthcoming); R. R. Reuther, *New Woman New Earth: Sexist Ideologies and Human Liberation* (New York, 1975).

17. Feminist Theologians therefore seek to revise liturgical language and to create new symbols and liturgies. See N. Morton, 'The Dilemma of Celebration', in C. Benedicks Fischer, B. Brenneman, A. McGrew Bennet (eds.) *Women in a Strange Land* (Philadelphia, 1975); A. Swidler, *Sistercelebrations. Nine Worship Experiences* (Philadelphia, 1974) has an excellent collection of feminist liturgies.

18. This is also emphasized by S. B. Ortner, in 'Is Female to Male as Nature is to Culture?', in M. Z. Rosaldo & L. Lamphere, *Woman, Culture and Society* (Stanford, 1974), pp. 67-87.

François Bussini

Changes in Theology and the New Contours of the Church's Catholicity

FOR SOME years people have glibly talked of the 'disintegration of Catholicism' or of 'shattered Christianity', and the symptoms on which they base their diagnosis have been catalogued exhaustively. And theology seems to be in a similar state: it consists of a jumble of writings on very diverse themes, themes suggested to their authors by their own awareness of cultural change, their political leanings, or their intellectual methods. This, at any rate, is how it appears. However, at least when one considers the French situation, one may conclude that there are certain lines of force dictating the changes in theology recorded in this *Concilium*. My purpose is to try to identify those lines of force.[1] We shall then see how, alongside those changes, the catholicity of the Church is taking on new contours, and we shall consider it, and how, those new contours enable the current theological renewal to confirm its fidelity to the same one Gospel.

A NEW THEOLOGICAL LANDSCAPE

The concern of all believers

Over the past ten years, theology has become less and less the preserve of specialist clergy. It has interested ever greater numbers of Christians. There is a significant minority of lay-people studying it in universities, and new study centres are coming into being and attracting a wide audience. The various Catholic Action groups now really set

33

out to do their own thinking when they reflect on the faith. If this trend continues, theology will become the business of all the faithful.

The pressing need for a hermeneutic

Such a change is not unrelated to the changes we can see in the aims of current research. For at the root of the new upsurge of interest in theology is the need to give an account of one's faith in a world where faith is no longer taken for granted. We have to ask ourselves precisely what we mean by adherence to Jesus Christ. By discovering just what is special about our faith, we hope to find reasons for persevering in it. But the trouble is that we have not got the words we need to answer the questions. Received standard Christian vocabulary has suffered a 'haemorrhage of meaning'.[2] The ideas it expresses are part of a doctrinal whole for which it is hard to find any echo in everyday experience. To rediscover the meaning of what we believe, we therefore seek to get beyond the language of the Church to Scripture itself. But difficulties at once present themselves. Is there any value in just sitting down to read Scripture? Will it not mean simply using the text as a basis for our own subjective meandering? Despite the uniqueness of these books, they seem so stamped by the age in which they were written that it is hard to see how documents from so distant a past can possibly have anything to say to us today.

To give an account of our faith we must once again make our own a meaning to which we have become strangers. A historical investigation of the sources is no longer enough—what those sources *say* must also take possession of us today. This will be possible only if their message finds an echo in the new problems posed by our own day-to-day experience. Only then can we really receive the Gospel and incarnate it in the way we live and speak. The theology of which Christians as a whole are coming to be the authors seeks above everything else to actualize the Christian message. It is a hermeneutics.

Verification

This theology is not generally the product of people working in isolation but of men and women seriously involved in catechesis, Catholic action, liturgical activities or the building up of communities. Furthermore, the experiences they examine to see whether they can echo the Gospel always include some degree of participation in the liberation struggles now rocking all our societies.

It is said that what people do validates the way they think and speak. Only critically comparing the Gospel with those liberation struggles shall we see whether for us, here and now, it is truly 'the power of God for salvation' (Rom 1:16). It seems clear, furthermore, that only our fellows can assure each of us our fidelity to that Gospel, and that the relationships among believers, under the overlordship of Jesus and his Spirit, prefigure the Kingdom to which we look forward in hope.

A FEW IN THE SERVICE OF ALL

Theology is becoming the concern of ever greater numbers of people, and professional theologians are gradually placing themselves at the service of this common task. The whole pace of their work is changing since it will be depending from now on on the study and reflexion of the laity. Indeed it seems that the hermeneutic endeavour, and the concern to find in the church's practice a confirmation of our profession of faith, have inspired all the most outstanding theological productions of recent years.

At the service of hermeneutics

The hermeneutic of the Gospel demands first of all that we give our attention to the completely new questions our experience faces us with. We must discover to what extent those questions prepare us to receive the apostolic message as a promise and a judgment applicable to us. But the questions themselves must also be analyzed and deepened. Every question always assumes a particular idea of the subject at issue, and such pre-suppositions can blur our vision and prevent our recognizing what is special to this particular thing.

Criticizing and deepening our questions

A great deal of work has been done that can help us to criticize the way in which we today question ourselves in relation to the Gospel. I can only mention a few instances here. We start by wondering what desire of our own impelled us to ask the question in the first place: for instance, it is important to know whether our studies about the resurrection could be motivated by a wish to avoid the ordeal of death, in which case we are in danger of by-passing the uniqueness of the message that he who was crucified is risen.[3] We must also try to be clear about the social position from which our reflexions start, thus countering the ideological threat that hangs over all religious discourse. We can see, for instance, how our concern for unanimity in the faith, and therefore for allowing a plurality of social options, might be based on a wish to disguise the class struggle which to some extent permeates the

Church, and so avoid having to take sides in it.[4] It has also been shown how a certain concept of the relationship between subject and object, and also the notion of truth as *adaequatio rei et intellectus*, have in the past stood in the way of a full acceptance of biblical eschatology.[5]

The way we question ourselves about the Gospel in the light of our experience needs criticizing, then, and our questions must also be made to go deeper. In effect what we have to find out is whether, and how, I, the subject of this or that experience can be subject to the offer of a covenant with God. Thus there are a lot of studies today about the possibility and the specialness of the act of faith. E. Levinas has led us to wonder under what circumstances it is conceivable and practicable for us to have a relationship with God, as genuinely distinct from the objects we deal with and the other people we confront. And it will be seen that such a relationship must of necessity be effected through our inescapable responsibility to other human beings.[6] There is a question too whether or not the various struggles for liberation that human beings have launched on their own initiative comprise any reference to a future that is coming to meet us because of the initiative of Another who is not a human being.[7] Since its object, via the mediation of Christ, is Another who is not a human being, the act of faith is unlike anything else. Henri de Lubac and H. Bouillard[8] among others have sought to re-emphasize the importance of the phrase, *Credere in Deum:* they remind us that the dogmas of faith can only be believed as long as there is a movement of one's entire being to assent to the overwhelming presence of God.

Towards creative faith

The reason for trying to understand our experience is to enable us to make the Gospel our own. It is in the nature of the Gospel to be 'delivered' and 'received' (cf. I Cor 15:1-5), but receiving the message means making it relevant here and now, and to do that one has to be continually moving between one cultural context and another. Such a movement is tending today to be the concern of everybody. Professional theologians provide the foundations for the work, demonstrating its necessity, and ensuring that it is rigorously carried out. They strive to bring alive the documents in which the Gospel is delivered to us and thus make them a mobilizing force.

For ten years now, larger numbers of Christians have been familiarizing themselves with historico-critical methods. They have grown accustomed to viewing Scripture as the crystallization of a history throughout which the events that marked the destiny of Israel, as well as the prophetic oracles that disclosed their meaning, have continually been commemorated and reinterpreted in terms of an ever-changing reality. Jesus, in his turn, presented an interpretation of the traditions of Israel in terms of his work and himself. Christians have received that interpretation as being God's final word (cf. Lk 24: 25-7; Acts 13:32; II Cor 1:20; Heb 1:1-2). But what God said once and for all, to all, has to be made our own by each one of us as we receive the apostolic message. As the New Testament demonstrates, it was a new process of living tradition that was opening.

The tradition of the Church is also to be put in historical perspective. This means that a number of the old ideas about the development of doctrine must be reviewed. It is hard to see doctrinal development as a continuous process analogous to biological maturing, for, in effect, problems keep changing throughout history, and there are manifold doctrinal 'structurings' to correspond to those changes.[9] These 'structurings' result from a combination of structuring elements drawn from the cultural environment (for instance, the use of the idea of *natura* to describe man as the object and recipient of proffered grace, or the doctrine of the 'two ends' of marriage), and 'structured' elements. These last include the explicit teachings of the kerygma as they have been differently stressed over the centuries, as well as the ideas about God and man presupposed by the relationship of the Covenant. These ideas are themselves thematized in varying ways. There can be no arithmetical equality among these different structurings (that is, between the terms and ideas taken individually), but only a proportional one. What you say in a particular doctrinal context, in the light of the problems that concern you, corresponds to what I say in the light of my problems, and the way they oblige me to think and to formulate the Gospel.

The Gospel is never delivered in isolation from such structurings. To make it one's own calls for an understanding of the structurings of the past that takes proper account of the approach to problems that they assume. It also calls for a re-structuring of what is received in the light of the specific problems and possibilities of each generation. This is as much the case with theological writing as it is with official dogmatic pronouncements.[10]

Historico-critical methods were based on the postulate that a complete identification or immediacy was possible between authors and readers via the texts. Readers who went carefully step-by-step through the processes of a document's production would rediscover, and could share in, the intentions of the writers. Today this assumption of the openness of language has been brought into question.[11] To start with, we are keenly aware that once a document is written, it becomes something separate from its author. It is then, in some sense, itself a signifier, because of the interplay among its internal elements. But that is precisely the trouble—there is a certain play, a certain flexibility, and the play will take a different character depending on the way the reader approaches the document. In other words, the mere fact of reading it is itself an interpretation of the message.

However they may differ, current approaches to Scripture and the documents of tradition still have the same effect. They all contribute to bringing them alive. The message suddenly becomes a moving force, and to receive it must then be a creative act. That act then becomes part of an everlasting process of reinterpreting and reactualizing the meaning of the events we commemorate when we say the Creed.

At the service of verification

All faith is therefore creative—but is all creativity faithful? The way the traditional message is reinterpreted will be based on the new questions posed by a new cultural framework, and by the history now being made in the various struggles for liberation. The Gospel will then once again be relevant. But is there not some danger of its losing its identity in the process? May we not end up with a 'tame Christianity in which the values of the Gospel, removed from their context, become for the most part no more than sources of rational argument and of energy for human struggles aimed at "penultimate" realities without reference to the "ultimate" reality that is Christ the Lord'?[12]

How ensure both the relevance *and* the identity of the Gospel? How verify current endeavours to reinterpret the message of salvation, to reformulate our faith? Those who are involved in the endeavours believe that they will find a way of verifying their work by creating a corporate 'us' of all Christians now engaged in history-in-the-making; and current research into the nature of the gospel truth would seem to confirm this idea.

The gospel message is quite precise. It says that the God of Abraham has raised up Jesus of Nazareth who was crucified, and made him Christ and Lord. All doctrinal theorizing must be measured against that fundamental statement.

But that good news can only be understood in relation to the Old Testament promises—promises confirmed once for all in the resurrection of the crucified Christ. In that, God has already fully realized the future promised to us all. Because of it, faith in God produces hope. We are moving towards the promised future, and in its name we reject the fixed disorder established under the sign of violence and idolatry. History is once again on the move. As J. Moltmann is forever reminding us, any reading of the Gospel that is dissociated from history in the making is bound to be a false reading.

Furthermore, as soon as we confess that Jesus is the Lord, we are sent back, like Mary Magdalen (Jn 20:11-18) and the two disciples on the road to Emmaus (Lk 24:13-35), to the community of our fellows that must be built up in the breaking of bread and the sharing of the good news. The same Spirit who makes us say 'Jesus, Lord' enables us to build up, each according to his own charism, a corporate 'us' in the Church, in which everyone hears and utters the same Gospel in their own language (cf. I Cor 12:14). And building it up makes it possible to confirm that the Spirit by whom God raised up Jesus is at work here and now. By fostering a communion among Jews and Greeks, slaves and freemen as so many human persons, the Spirit overcomes the forces of death that would shut off each individual in relentless solitude.[13] This 'us' of the Church prefigures the future of the Kingdom in whose name we combat the established disorder. This 'us' is indeed the point of verification for every interpretation of the one Gospel in deed or word.

COMMUNION AMONG THE CHURCHES—THE WORK OF THE SPIRIT

Only as long as it is accompanied by the building up of the ecclesial 'us' can the current theological renewal remain faithful to the one Gospel and keep its promises. It is vital also that the way this 'us' is conceived and realised should correspond to those promises.

Two lines of force in the theology of the Church

A quick look at the present drift of ecclesiology shows that there is indeed such a correspondence.

1. *Restoring the Trinitarian basis of ecclesiology.* We are trying today to emerge from the narrowness of what has been called the 'Christo-monist schema'.[14] In this perspective, the Church grows out of one continuous process. Everything starts with Christ, who gives the apostles power to govern and to teach, and the apostles in turn hand on that power to the bishops. The blessings of salvation are then passed on to the people *via* their pastors. But this is a very incomplete view, and is likely to leave us thinking that the people are no more than the passive objects of government and teaching. This interpretation has to be fitted into a larger vision—which appears once one gives ecclesiology its Trinitarian basis. This means giving its full weight to the statement in the Creed that presents the Church as a creation of the Spirit. Not only does he lead us to Christ, so that in him and through him we should have access to the Father (Eph 2:18); the Spirit also causes us to gather into that communion of persons I have just spoken

of. But the construction and the mission of that Church are the concern
of all Christians, each taking a share in the common task according to
his own charism. All become one whole in the Church. But for *all* to
become that whole, *some* must be specifically and permanently responsible for those vital functions of the Church—communion in faith,
bearing witness to the Gospel, and the service of those in need.[15] This
is not just empty theorizing. As I have said, *all* of us are tending
towards becoming involved in theological thinking, but that is only a
possibility because *some* of us place our resources, of nature and of
grace, at the service of the common task.

2. *Re-evaluating the local church.* It is in the here-and-now that the
Church is taking shape, that it preaches the Gospel and serves the
poor. This is what emerges clearly from the second line of force of
current ecclesiology. We are in fact re-evaluating the importance of
individual churches.[16] As soon as the people in any place gather together in response to the Gospel to proclaim the Lord's death and life
by the logic of their belief in the new covenant, then the mystery of the
one and only Church of God is itself present there.[17]

This being so, cultural distinctions are important from the very first.
We do not start with a generalized doctrinal or institutional order,
which is then applied specifically according to the locality. From the
start the Church is born and develops in a vital relationship with its
cultural context. Obviously no church is ever constructed *ex nihilo*. It
always receives the Gospel that unites it from some other church. But
receiving the Gospel is precisely setting in motion that creative faith I
have spoken of. And it is that faith that enables every individual church
to confess one and the same good news in words and actions that are
truly its own.

THE DOCTRINAL RESPONSIBILITY OF PASTORS

A particular church is fully the one Church of God here and now in
so far as it is in communion with other churches. Now, it is clear from a
true understanding of what ordination means[18] that the work of the
bishop, and his collaborators, the priests, is to serve just this Catholic
communion. In doing so, they play the specific and indispensable rôle
of presiding over the worship of the new covenant. Similarly, they also
have a specific doctrinal task to perform. To understand what this task
involves, we must consider two of the theological points I have
mentioned.

The 'Christo-monist' schema led naturally enough to making the
magisterium of the pastors the 'immediate rule' of faith. The faithful
had first of all to receive the teaching of the magisterium. Theology

then stepped in to show how Scripture and tradition proved the validity of that teaching.[19] But, in the more holistic view that now prevails, what is basic is the action of the Church, here and now, invoking the Holy Spirit in each of its members, to give them all to 'know whom they believe' (II Tim 1:12). That *Ecclesia* is inscribed in the continuity of living Tradition by receiving Scripture in an act of creative faith. The clergy are at the service of this common task of all believers.

To specify the service proper to them, we must remember a second point. As I have said, the truth of the Gospel is a call to serve the liberation of those in trouble, and to build up the fraternal community. On the ecclesiological level, this inward link between truth and *agape* is expressed by a kind of interweaving of the mark of apostolicity with that of catholicity. Let me give an example from Acts (an example to which Luke gives a normative value), to explain what I mean. The church in Antioch contained both Jews and Greeks (Acts 11:19-22), and had a character of its own that was quite different from the church in Jerusalem. Its ministerial organization was apparently special, and it became a missionary centre to which Paul and Barnabas were attached (Acts 13:1-3). To preach the Gospel to the Gentiles called for a profound re-thinking of the primitive kerygma. First, there must be a tremendous stress on monotheism as a necessary first principle, while less importance was to be given to the evidence of Scripture.[20] It was also important to indicate that Christianity was something quite new and different as compared with the tradition of Israel; it was also vital for the Christians there to have a thorough understanding of Hellenistic culture and be able to offer a radical critique of it. But in proportion as they became different from one another, the churches of Antioch and Jerusalem strengthened the bonds of communication and discussion between them (Acts 13:3; 15), as well as of practical help (Paul's famous collection). In this paradigmatic case we see how communion between the churches and fidelity to the primordial witness of the twelve went hand in hand. The church in Antioch and the churches connected with it were only true churches of God in so far as they were recognized by Jerusalem. Jerusalem held the memory of the founding experience of Cephas and the apostles (cf. Gal 1:18; I Cor 15:5). But, on the other hand, Jerusalem would only be faithful to the Gospel of the apostles if it approved and supported the bold missionaries of Antioch in doctrinal and institutional matters. In other words, communion verified apostolicity. Conversely, no communion was possible without a faithful and living memory of the witness of Cephas and the others.

In view of the various points I have recalled, it seems to me that the doctrinal duty of the clergy involves two complementary and inseparable aspects.

First, they must foster catholicity to make it possible to validate new formulations of the faith.

That catholicity must, of course, be fostered within each individual church. While encouraging the initiatives of the faithful and facilitating the work of professional theologians, agencies for comparison will develop. In this way, the various formulations of the faith can criticize one another, and the proportional equality I mentioned earlier will be confirmed (that is, seeing whether it is so, and making it so). Those formulations will then gradually become creeds, 'symbols'—in short, signs of recognition among Christians.

The more the different churches define their singularities, the more lively will be the exchanges among them. In such exchanges, each bishop will make clear to the other churches the way in which his church bears witness to the one Gospel in its own particular context. Conversely, the bishop will get his church to share in the problems and the efforts of the other churches. It is the role of the Church of Rome and its bishop to preside over this communion of churches.

The clergy must also watch to see that their churches are faithful to the apostolic 'deposit', so as to ensure the cohesion of the Catholic communion.

All tradition attests that this duty of vigilance is imprescriptible. But the end in view will normally determine how it is exercised. How is this duty to be understood and carried out today? In the space of an article, I can only give a few of what seem to me the most important elements of reply.

It is not for the clergy to impose, from outside so to say, their own ready-made teaching upon the faithful. They must seek rather to exercise a sort of controlling action, and to discern the authenticity or otherwise of the work whereby Christians are now trying to reformulate the Gospel and make it once more their own.

This brings us to the delicate problem of the criteria of such discernment, and in this sphere, the closest possible collaboration between pastors and professional theologians is indispensable.

I would stress again the decisiveness of the criterion of catholicity. Once a Christian initiative develops the kind of logic that makes its authors become more and more antipathetic to all exchanges and resent arrangements for mutual criticism, then it seems to me that the evangelical quality of the initiative is problematic.

Among Christians today there is a catholicity that mocks at distance. There is also a catholicity in time, so that the dogmatic formulations that regulated unanimity in the past remain normative in our own day. Nevertheless, 'the authority of a dogmatic formula is not exercised in the same way towards its contemporaries as towards succeeding generations'.[21] As I have said, the problems change. Dogmatic formulations can only fulfil their function to the extent that one perceives both exactly what they meant when they were first stated, and what is different about the problems of today. To receive statements of this kind one must of necessity re-interpret and re-formulate them.

To appreciate in themselves the new formulations of faith, one must consider to what extent they obey the great laws of balance on which the solidity of the covenant economy depends. Let me recall briefly a few of the most obvious: a complementarity between Christology 'from below' and Christology 'from above'; subordination of the demands of the law to the promptings of grace, with both being seen in the light of God's promises and opening a future vista to those to whom they are addressed; a schema that constitutes a 'berakah' to serve as a memorial of the Lord for the eucharistic liturgy; a Trinitarian-based ecclesiology. These laws represent something of the richness and the uniqueness of the figure of Christ the Lord. And they shape the actions and words of those who, by the power of the Spirit, become the Lord's vassals.

It thus becomes clear that, as I see it, pastoral discernment is directed to guiding, but also to stimulating that hermeneutical endeavour that is the concern of everyone. That is why it is important for pastors to watch carefully how their interventions are 'received'. Its reception is not what confers legitimacy on any pastoral act, but it does determine its effectiveness.[22] Some clerical initiatives are a dead letter from the start, whereas others are really constructive. They add impetus and assurance to a renewal in depth of the spiritual life. Watching the process of their reception enables one to measure the relevance of one's decisions. It shows whether the points of reference one has suggested really relate to the particular problems posed by these particular people. The quality of reception also presents a good way of diagnosing how effectively the Catholic communion is functioning. For really, when it comes to doctrine, as with everything else, the pastor will fulfil his rôle *for* the service of his church all the better if he will travel the road patiently along *with* it.

The purpose of the pastor's watchfulness over doctrine is Catholic communion, and indeed to ensure communion there must be such a ministry. By positioning himself in such a way as to make sure that his church is attentive to other churches and aware of the fact that the gospel of grace is always the same, the pastor helps his church to rid itself of all narcissism and self-sufficiency. He reminds the sinners who compose it that they are only gathered together in response to the summons of Another who is ready to forgive us and to take possession of us, giving us to himself in the dead and risen Christ. As H. Denis writes, 'to draw a line round doctrine at one particular point in history is a way of drawing a line round the assembly of believers'.[23] It is in so far as the Church 'knows whom it believes' that it will bear the imprint of its Lord and be able to speak for the whole world.

This account of the present situation has undoubtedly been very selective. However, the lines of force that seem to emerge from it are hopeful. The hope will prove justified if the ecclesial renewal and the theological renewal now going on continue to enrich and verify one another.

Translated by Rosemary Sheed

Notes

1. This study owes much to Institut Catholique de Paris, *Recherches actuelles III, Le déplacement de la théologie* (*Le Point Théologique*, 21) (Paris, 1977); H. Denis, *Les chemins de la théologie dans le monde de ce temps* (Paris, 1977); J. Hoffmann, 'Französische Theologie heute', *Theologische Qartalschrift* 153 (1973), pp. 54-67.

2. G. Widmer, 'Sens ou non-sens des énoncés théologiques', *Revue de Sciences Philosophiques et Théologiques* 51 (1967), p. 652.

3. See J. Moltmann, *Umkehr zur Zukunft* (Munich, 1970); J. Pohier, 'Un cas de foi post-freudienne à la resurrection?', in *Concilium* 105 (1975), pp. 115-30.

4. See J. Guichard, *Eglise, lutte des classes et stratégies politiques* (Paris, 1972); A. Durand, *Pour une Eglise partisane* (Paris, 1974).

5. See J. Moltmann, *Theology of Hope* (London & New York, 1966).

6. See E. Levinas, 'Dieu et la philosophie', *Le Nouveau Commerce*, 30-31 (1975), pp. 97-128; G. Petitdemange, 'Ethique et transcendance, Sur les chemins d'E. Levinas', *Recherches de Science Religieuse* 64 (1976), pp. 59-64.

7. This was the subject at issue in the debate between E. Bloch and J. Moltmann, *Theology of Hope*, op. cit.

8. H. de Lubac, *La foi chretienne, Essai sur la structure du Symbole des Apôtres* (Paris, 1969), pp. 131-68, 285-348; H. Bouillard, *Comprendre ce que l'on croit* (Paris, 1971), pp. 125-50.

9. See J. P. Jossua, 'Immutabilité, progrès ou structurations multiples des doctrines chrétiennes?', in *Revue des Sciences Philosophiques et Théologiques*, 52 (1968) pp. 173-200. Jossua's word 'structuration' could perhaps be elucidated and its use justified once more today.

10. In this connection see E. Schillebeeckx, in *Concilium* (1973).

11. This questioning seems to me to lie at the root of the new approaches that are described somewhat summarily as methods of structural analysis.

12. Mgr R. Etchegaray, 'Rapport sue l'Eglise en Europe', presented to the episcopal synod held in Rome in 1974, in *L'Eglise des cinq continents* (Paris, 1975), p. 103.

13. On the inward interrelationship of truth, charity and life, see L. Bouyer, *L'Eglise de Dieu* (Paris, 1970), pp. 315-23, 401-48.

14. See H. Legrand, 'Synodes et Conseils de l'après-concile', *Nouvelle Revue Theologique*, 98 (1976), p. 201; Y. Congar, *Ministères et communion ecclésiale* (Paris, 1971), pp. 9-49.

15. On the dialectic of 'all' and 'some', see J. Delorme, 'Diversité et unité des ministères d'après le Nouveau Testament', in *Le ministère et les ministères selon le Nouveau Testament* (Paris, 1974), pp. 283-346; B. Sesboüé, 'Ministères et structure de l'Eglise', ibid., pp. 347-417.

16. This re-evaluation is based primarily on the decree *Christus Dominus* of Vatican II. Cf. the commentary by H. Legrand in *La charge pastorale des évêques*, text, translation and commentaries (*Unam Sanctum*, 74) (Paris, 1969), pp. 104-23. See also the same author in *Concilium* (1972).

17. On the various levels of realization of individual churches, see F. Bussini, 'Donner lieu à l'Eglise', *Lumière et Vie*, 123 (1975), pp. 60-72.

18. See H. Legrand, *La charge pastorale des èvêques*, pp. 108-13.

19. See B. Sesboüé, 'Autorité du Magistère et vie de foi ecclésiale', *Nouvelle Revue Théologique*, 93 (1971), pp. 338-45; Y. Congar, in *Concilium* (1973).

20. In this connection one may compare I Cor 15:3-5, which echoes the earliest preaching, with I Thess 1:9-10, the formula worked out for the mission to the pagans; or similarly, the various discourses to the Jews in Acts 2 to 15, with the preaching to the Athenians in Acts 17.

21. B. Sesboüé, 'Autoritè du Magistère', pp. 354-55.

22. See Y. Congar, 'La réception comme réalité ecclésiologique', *Revue des Sciences Philosophiques et Théologiques*, 56 (1972), pp. 369-403.

23. *L'Evangile et les dogmes* (in the series *Croire et Comprendre*) (Paris, 1974), p. 138.

Klaus Ahlheim

'A Question of Human Life and Dignity': How Theology Changes in Social Conflicts

'FOR A society based on the production of commodities, in which the producers in general enter into social relations with one another by treating their products as commodities and values, whereby they reduce their individual private labour to the standard of homogeneous human labour—for such a society, Christianity, with its *cultus* of abstract man . . . is the most fitting form of religion.'[1]

The situation described by Karl Marx in this passage as 'the cultus of abstract man' still conditions most books and theories produced by Western European, and especially German, theology, which, on the rare occasions on which it takes any notice of ecumenical theology and its positions, does so hesitantly and as an exotic exception. Our theologizing is still concerned with Man with a capital M, whose fundamental philosophical locus is only accidentally affected by historical change, Man in his unchanging essence, seen moreover first as an individual, independent of the pressures exerted on his will by his social environment. And even when theology deals specifically with questions of social ethics, we rarely hear anything about the specific problems of workers, about solidarity in labour disputes and industrial struggles, about stoppages and strikes. Apart from a few timid experiments in theology in such places as industrial missions, the Church and theology still stop at the factory gate. This means that on the whole

46

theology and the Church treat the majority of the population—and the majority of the Church's members—with their worries, problems and conflicts, their wishes and their dreams, as almost non-existent.

I

'Please contact your delegates, the IGM committee, . . . or *one of the presbyteries* with details of when you are prepared to distribute bulletins and what resources . . . you can provide' (emphasis added). A short but significant item from the metal union's 'News for VFW Fokker, Speyer Plant', published in 1976.[2] Delegates of the work force, trade union officials and parish priests in what is hardly a customary alliance, firmly on the side of those who are required to lose their jobs by the higher logic of economic profitability. Christian defence minister Georg Leber (Fokker, like the rest of the aviation industry, lives off government orders and public money) explains this logic with blunt realism: 'In their internal planning companies must base decisions on company structure on economic considerations.'[3] From the point of view of a 'top dog', it's simply obvious. But the Catholic workers' movement in Speyer, the parish priests and even Ernst Gutting, the town's auxiliary bishop, have adopted the viewpoint of the 'underdogs' and opposed the management's cynical policy. 'This firm doesn't care about the victims, about the people involved,' declared one priest,[4] who didn't want to leave it at statements: 'This firm has already put itself in breach of the law! Faced with this situation, the workers must also experiment with new forms of struggle to resist these measures!'[5] The issue of the distribution of property, normally taboo, arose almost inevitably: 'We're too nice about it! According to the constitution property brings social responsibilities. Let's take that as a guideline for the coming struggle!'[6]

In Speyer many of the Protestant and Catholic clergy sided with the victims of an industrial policy which on its own terms appeared logical but was in reality inhuman. This not only altered the relationship of the so-called laity to the Church, but also affected the way the clergy thought of themselves theologically. Their intervention in the conflict altered their social position. They had lost their illusory position of being above social conflicts and instead very quickly found themselves on one side in the social struggle. Questions about the justification of our property structure and the structure of our society in general arose logically, almost inevitably. They were bound up with the realization that human dignity (not some abstract, unhistorical dignity, but dignity in real situations of ordinary life, at work, in one's position as an employee, in the family, in everyday situations) had to be the cornerstone of all theological thinking and the goal of all the Church's actions.

Whenever—which, in West Germany at least, is not very often—official representatives of the Church give up their apparent neutrality, which is in fact support for the status quo, they have similar experiences.

Take Bruchsal, where a struggle to save jobs in the Siemens plant has been going on for two years. Protestant and Catholic clergy refused to keep silent, and talked at services about the threatened loss of jobs, and also helped families faced with the worry of unemployment. In September 1976, 6,000 people marched through Bruchsal, and they included twenty-five of the thirty local Catholic priests. According to trade union representatives, the priests had realized that it was wrong 'for a firm to have so much power if the result was to be such tragedies'.[7]

In March 1977 twelve Catholic priests belonging to the deanery of Saarbrücken-Malstatt-Burbach issued a public statement from the pulpit about proposed mass dismissals at the Neunkirchen and Vöklingen-Burbach steelworks. Reaction was mixed: on the one hand friendly advice to drop the subject, and even hints about a Vatican shareholding in the firms concerned,[8] and on the other rage. The twelve priests were quickly labelled 'red' and 'communist'. Here again the clergy had said, 'If the present economic system is unable to guarantee people their fundamental existential right to work, we must question it and change it.'[9] This questioning is based on a thoroughly anthropocentric, but nevertheless biblically based theology.

This comes out very clearly in another example, the appeal of five priests to the DEMAG management in Duisburg in 1975. Here too the closure of the Kalldorf plant was to lead to the destruction of six hundred jobs, once more as part of a long-term commercial plan. The five theologians' reaction was sharp and clear: 'When Jesus Christ says, "Man was not made for the sabbath, but the sabbath for man," he is also saying that man does not exist for the economy, but the economy for man, and that means that the employee was not made for the firm, but the firm for human beings.

'In the case of the Kalldorf plant it seems to us that human beings are not controlling the firm, but the firm and money are controlling human beings. When the good of man, whom God willed to be his image, does not come first, it is replaced by the power of anonymous economic structures which are rooted in the selfishness of people who, for their own advantage, have little hesitation in neglecting the interests of their fellow men. This applies to a management just as much as to workers and each one of us.

'We intend to work in our own spheres of influence, in our parishes and parish councils, to ensure that, in accordance with God's will, man becomes the centre of our actions and words.'[10] The regional synod of Lippe also supported the appeal to the firm of DEMAG-Mannesmann 'to put the welfare of human beings first in all its planning and decisions.'[11]

In 1973, during the strike at the Mannesmann foundry at Huckingen, near Duisburg, more than fifty Protestant and Catholic clergy issued a statement of solidarity, and incurred the wrath of the bosses by their support for the working population. A letter of solidarity from the council of theology students in the Rhineland to sacked Mannesmann workers contained the following passage: 'As theology students, we intend to work and fight in the Church to ensure that it does not go on being simply the Church of the rulers, of the well-to-do and the bourgeoisie. The socialist movement must be brought into the Church because the Church is under the power of the same enemy. The law of competition and company profit is not the law of Jesus Christ, which runs: "bear one another's burdens"!'[12]

These examples from West Germany show the beginnings of timid tendencies which point towards a different theology and a different Church. This Church really takes human beings seriously in their actual existence, in their work and their everyday lives, and the tendencies also expose a theology which pretends to work on a level above social contradictions as what it really is, a supplier of ideology for the status quo.

II

It is no accident that such developments took on sharper definition in a labour dispute which was headline news in *France* for several months, the struggle for the Lip watch factory in Besançon. It is also central to our discussion and will therefore be described in detail. Lip revealed the first signs—but enough to worry the ruling class—of a different Church and a different Christianity, and perhaps also a sort of 'implicit' theology based on the fundamental, though often suppressed, realization that Christian faith—whatever its detailed definition—and daily life under capitalist conditions are as compatible as fire and water.

Although the government and the employers constantly denounced the forms and strategies of the Lip struggle as illegal, ministers of the Church showed solidarity with the fighting workers in practical and effective ways.

At the climax of the dispute, when the para-military emergency police, the CRS (élite units hardened in numerous strikes and demonstrations) had occupied the factory, the Lip workers voted to continue production elsewhere. Components which had previously been stockpiled were used, and a small watchmaking industry was set up under the slogan 'The factory is where the people are.'

Following the local council, the Catholic clergy now made rooms available to the strikers. The daily meetings were held in a cinema belonging to the Church, and committees met in the Pius X church. Church dignitaries took part in the mass demonstration against the police occupation of the factory. In the hunt for the so-called war-chest (a hidden stock of watches put by as a bargaining counter) parts of Besançon cathedral and even the cold store of a monastery were searched.

Marc Lallier, archbishop of Besançon and reputed to be of conservative leanings, supported the Lip workers in a statement read in churches. He denounced the way in which decisions were taken over the heads of those affected, and ended: 'God's will is that everyone should be able to live by his work. It is, as we say today, job security.'[13] Critics of such partiality by a churchman did not hesitate to dismiss Lallier as a 'red bishop'. Lallier replied, 'Remarkable utterances, which I have never made, have been attributed to me. To form an accurate opinion, people must read the three texts published here. If they show that I am a "red bishop", well, I cannot deny what I have written. Nevertheless it does not stop me holding to my view that our present social injustices cannot be abolished by anything short of revolution, which will involve violence. . . .

'I have been described as a dreamer who supports the Lip workers unconditionally, when economic pressures meant that sooner or later two or three hundred of them would have to be sacked.

'Whatever people say, I do not reject economic necessities . . . but I am still forced to watch the necessity of dismissals being insisted on after four months of conflict.

'I said that people should imagine what a sacked worker goes through and that one should do everything possible to avoid it. Violence should be avoided at all costs, which means that people must seek agreement and not refuse concessions. This is the limit of my "support", but to that limit it is genuine. I believe in all modesty that my responsibility as a bishop lays on me the obligation to remind everyone of this urgent duty. Have I been a greater dreamer than Jesus Christ?'[14]

Among observers of the most varied political background confusion reigned. What was for the enlightened critics of one side simply impossible, and for the interests of the other in maintaining the status quo unacceptable, had happened at Lip. Christians had taken sides in the class struggle, for the exploited, dominated and oppressed. *Le Monde* complained in despair: 'A divided Church . . . . All those who have been in the forefront of the Lip conflict for six months are all avowed Christians, and particularly active ones, *but they are in different camps.*'[15]

If coping with such clear support from Church circles for the militant Lip workers created particular problems for West German commentators, an assessment of the Catholic left traditions which had had at least a marginal influence on the Lip conflict was totally beyond their powers. A. Münster, in his book on the Lip dispute, comments simply that since its change of name in 1964 the CFDT had 'moved steadily further away from its Christian traditions'.[16] In fact it can be seen that the separation from the official Catholic Church liberated social revolutionary elements of the Catholic tradition and allowed them to become much more influential. And these elements, in any case, had always been one of the influences in the French working-class movement.

It is true that 1964 was a significant moment in the history of what had hitherto been the CFTC, but not in the sense that previously the Christian tradition had been everything and afterwards there was only socialism. It was during the Resistance that the CFTC had first begun to move to an anti-capitalist position, but after the Liberation this was taken no further. There was a worker-priest movement, but this was stopped again by the hierarchy in 1953. And after the Second World War there was a Catholic left tradition whose theoretical disputes were reflected in the periodicals *Jeunesse de l'Eglise* and *Témoignage Chrétien*. The question whether there was a connection between capitalism and the decline of faith was unavoidable, and to many it seemed clear 'that the system of human relations which (capitalism) has created has multiplied the unfavourable objective conditions for the development of a world of free men and a universe of believers. . . . A real renewal of the Church . . . cannot take place unless the exploitation of man by man is first totally abolished.'[17]

There is no doubt that elements from a Catholic left tradition played a part in the Lip workers' struggle. They were not central, they do not adequately explain such an important stage in the history of the working-class movement as the struggle of the Lip workers, but they were in some way a natural part of it.

The statements of Lip workers and the reasons they give, often only in passing, for their action reveal two quite clear attitudes. Scepticism about the poltical activity of the institutional Church goes with continued adherence to social revolutionary strands of Christian tradition which have persisted in spite of the official Church's predominant role as a support for systems of authority.

Criticism of the official Church and ordinary parish life is not based on abstract theological or political principles, but supported by direct everyday experience. A CFDT delegate, for example, said, 'I'm a Christian, more and more, but I practise less and less. The reason is simple. I can't bring myself to pray in church side by side with an employer who exploits me during the week. Take my own community. I can think of three bosses and several directors of factories there. They may be in the parish, but they're blind to everything that concerns their firm.'[18] This account by a woman worker at Lip is also illuminating: 'The next day I said I would go to mass with Mother, not so much out of religious conviction as to please my mother, to see the people from the village again, to bring back memories of my childhood in the little church. I believe in God and in some of the teachings of Christianity, but I regret all the distortions for which the Church has been responsible through the centuries. And all the gold is wrong, the finery; it doesn't correspond to what Christ taught, and that's the basis of our religion. And the way people were brainwashed! For generations they lived in fear of a strict God, tortured in body and mind because they thought they'd fallen into sin because of some little mistakes.

'Although the Church glorifies the woman as mother in the family, it denigrates women and forces them into a humiliating and degrading rôle in relation to men. The charity they preach about is turned into its opposite. The person who practises it feels proud, but the person who's the object of it feels humiliated. Too many Catholics soothe their consciences by giving alms, and think they're being generous when they pity the poor. That's too comfortable. It's just what enables the powerful to control the people. Give the poor just enough to keep them from starving, see the gratitude in their eyes, pay the workers badly, leave the peasants just a little profit, and the small shopkeepers just enough for them to accept their lot, din into them that they're well off if they bear their sufferings without getting rebellious. That's the right way to keep power. Happy are the poor.'[19]

Statements which indicate a positive relation to the Christian tradition also stay close to everyday life and activity. They don't contain theology, or even politics with a theological trimming; they are simply reports of the different experiences people have had as Christians or of the way others experience them. Charles Piaget, for example, now perhaps one of the best-known CFDT representatives, active in the Catholic workers' movement and a member of the PSU (Partie socialiste unifié), gives the following answer to the question how he sees his faith in Jesus Christ in relation to his political activities: 'There are the meetings of the Catholic workers' organization, where we bring up the various problems that face us. Then there's the way we go about trade union work. You try not to forget the human beings involved. It's not easy. You tend to react to force by letting yourself go. We try to avoid getting caught up in that process. We tell ourselves that the other side are human beings. The comrades have often said to us, ''You can see straight away that you're Christians.'' And yet we agree with the Marxist and Communist comrades on a particular view of man. They come to it through a schema, through thinking, we through our faith.'[20]

Piaget, the Christian comrade, who doesn't like being called a workers' leader, grew up in a family of practising Catholics, who tended to be right-wing in politics. He himself says he was brought to the political left by meetings of the Catholic workers' organization, and especially by the experiences of the problems and sufferings brought by the war in Algeria. He has remained a practising Catholic, and feels—partly as a result of the solidarity of the official Church during the Lip struggle—more comfortable in the Church than in the past. 'I think there has been a very significant move. Fifteen years ago we didn't feel quite comfortable in the Church, and that's not true any more. I don't think the Church has changed completely, but it's moving. And of course one can't say that everything's already been achieved. We're just on the move, back to the sources. And in the end I'm an optimist. You go forward, and can take advantage of what you've already achieved. The fight at Lip would have been unthinkable ten years ago. It was perhaps in advance of the time, but it was only possible because May '68 took place, because there had been a renewal in the Church, in union work and in politics.'[21]

The Lip workers' amazing slogan, 'Anything is possible,' proclaimed on thousands of posters, not only indicates the utopian dimension of the ordinary battle, but was also a reality in their experiments with new forms. 'The thing about this dispute which made the biggest impression on me,' one woman remembers, 'is what I'd call warmth, something in discussions which wasn't there before. Relationships became friendly, whereas before there were just contacts at work. People used to talk about quotas, about work. Now they talk about relations between people at work, and that's a big difference. For me, as a Christian, human relationships are the most important thing. People are discovering themselves, discovering that there are such things as friendships, love, solidarity. We've learnt a lot in this dispute. We've learnt what life is, what a human being is, and the respect due to a human being. We learnt a lot, and we can go on living with it, in one way or another, at Lip or somewhere else. I'm going to carry on.'[22]

One must be extremely cautious about drawing general conclusions from these rough descriptions, but an interim assessment of initiatives and tendencies is both possible and important.

III

In the labour disputes and industrial conflicts we have described the ministers of the Church who became involved in the social conflicts changed their theological attitude. The change also affected the associated political choices, and the identification with the existing social system, which had often been taken for granted, was called in question, while theological language and Christian action were forced to become partisan. For the institutional Church this may initially be no more than a marginal phenomenon.

But the people involved, the striking and fighting workers, not only experienced unexpected solidarity on the part of the Church; they also came to have new, almost subtle experiences with elements of the Christian tradition, elements which were not even always called Christian or regarded as Christian. They didn't produce a new theology, nor did they have a sense of being a different, alternative Christian community. And yet Christian tradition was almost taken for granted as one element, not in the word preached, spoken or written, but in the shared experience of struggle, in ways of behaving towards other people, in new personal relationships. At this point academic theology may despair, and ask in superior tones for the *proprium*, the distinctively Christian element, but the very question shows that it lacks the equipment to perceive and assimilate such experiences.

Workers fighting for jobs are involved with the 'question of human life and dignity';[23] that this is also a theological question is obvious. 'Anything is possible'—perhaps the background of changed experiences in political struggle gives new relevance to biblical sayings such as that from Mark's gospel, 'All things are possible to him who believes' (Mk 9:23). First, though, the political explosiveness of this process must be recognised and accepted. It appears again in Bishop Lallier's words, 'Anything which mutilates human beings . . . is contrary to God's plan.'[24]

Translated by Francis McDonagh

Notes

1. Karl Marx, *Capital,* vol. I, Lawrence and Wishart (London, 1970), p. 79.
2. *Metall. Nachrichten für VFW Fokker, Werk Speyer,* No. 7, 12.3.1976.
3. *Publik-Forum,* 21.2.1976, p. 10.
4. *Metall. Nachrichten für VFW-Fokker,* No. 8, 15.3.1976.
5. Ibid.
6. Ibid.
7. Cf. *Frankfurter Rundschau,* 30 April 1977.
8. Cf. ibid.
9. Ibid.
10. *'Wir kämpfen um unsere Arbeitsplätze', Dokumentation der Belegschaft DEMAG-Kunststofftechnik, Kalldorf (Lippe) 1969-1975,* published by Industriegewerkschaft Metall für die Bundesrepublik Deutschland, Bezirksleitung Münster, p. 31.
11. Ibid., p. 32.
12. D. Sölle and K. Schmidt, eds., *Christen für den Sozialismus,* vol. I (Stuttgart, 1975), p. 50.
13. *Le Monde,* 7.9.73.
14. *Le Monde,* 31.10.73 (emphasis added).
15. A. Münster, *Der Kampf bei Lip. Arbeiterselbstverwaltung in Frankreich* (Berlin, West, 1974), p. 15. In 1964 the Confédération Française des Travailleurs Chrétiens (CFTC) changed its name to Confédération Française Démocratique du Travail (CFDT). For the issues involved, see the two books by F. Krumnow, *Croire ou le feu de la vie* (Paris, 1975) and *CFDT au coeur* (Paris, 1976).
16. H. Lange, *Wissenschaftlich-technische Intelligenz. Neue Bourgeoisie oder neue Arbeiterklasse?* (Cologne, 1972), p. 189.
17. Ibid., p. 189.
18. Roland Vittot, CFTD delegate, quoted from *LIP—Charles Piaget et les LIP racontent* (Paris, 1973), pp. 123-24.
19. M. Piton, *Anders leben. Chronik eines Arbeitskampfes: Lip, Besançon* (Frankfurt am Main, 1976), pp. 18-19.
20. *Témoignage Chrétien,* 30.8.1973.
21. Ibid.
22. *Lip Unité,* October 1974.
23. According to an editorial in *Lip actualité,* Oct. 1977.
24. From the archbishop's statement of 3 June 1973 mentioned above.

PART II

New Cultural Factors

Bas van Iersel

The Exegete and Linguistics

A PERSONAL MEMORY

THE BIBLICAL exegete may well be influenced in his attitude towards linguistically orientated exegesis by the way in which he is first brought into contact with linguistics as such. To illustrate this, I will begin this article with a personal memory. Leaving aside instances that apply only to the Netherlands,[1] my first contact with linguistics can be dated almost exactly. It took place at the annual meeting of the central committee of *Concilium* in Paris in May 1967. As usual, there was a press conference on this occasion and this took place at the Institut Catholique. The journalists and younger theologians were less interested in what was being said by a panel of *Concilium* theologians and only anxious to hear what the members of that panel thought about structuralism. In fact, most of the members had at that time hardly heard of structuralism. Most of them, moreover, tended to think of it as a fashionable and ephemeral French phenomenon. (I am bound to add in self-defence that, even in France, very few theologians had much idea at that time of the importance that structuralism might have for our knowledge of the Bible in particular.) It was not until 1969 that the first symposium of biblical scholars and structuralists took place[2] and, as far as I know, there were, before 1970, no publications in which scriptural texts were subjected to structural analysis.

I must at once add that it would be wrong to think of linguistics and structuralism as identical. On the one hand, structuralism is also concerned with non-linguistic objects of research. On the other, linguistics

59

include other approaches apart from those of structuralism. Nonetheless, I feel bound to mention this incident in Paris as my first contact with linguistics, even though it was a contact that revealed a shortcoming. At the same time, contemporary linguistics and the current structuralist analysis of language and literary texts have a great deal in common. Let us look at the most important of these similarities.

In both models, there is little or no interest in diachronic aspects, that is, the development through which a language or a text passes. Interest is almost exclusively directed towards the synchronic aspects, that is, towards the language or text that is given at a particular time. In the case of linguistics, this has led to a noticeable decline in interest in the historical aspect of language and etymology. In the case of biblical scholarship, it has led to a neglect of every attempt to say anything about the development or history of a text or any part of a text. There is therefore no place in this model of research for such studies as form criticism or the history of traditions and the editing of biblical texts. There are several examples of strong opposition to these current methods of research.

A second characteristic of both models is a predominant concern for underlying structures. Both linguists and structuralists are preoccupied, not with the visible organization of the grammatical meaning or the content of a text, but rather with the deeper connections at a more abstract level and the way in which the concrete meaning or text is produced from this. To express this in a more technical way, there is more interest in the inner structure than in the sequence of the parts of the meaning or the text.

A third feature common to both linguistics and structuralism is an unmistakable tendency to work towards a universal theory that can be applied to all languages and all texts that exist or may exist.

My first genuine and positive acquaintance with linguistics and structuralism was made through the medium of a number of publications in which linguistics were applied to the analysis and exegesis of biblical texts. These appeared about 1970 in various countries.[3] The most important of these in the German-speaking countries were the books and articles (especially in the journal *Linguistica Biblica*) by E. Güttgemanns and his circle.[4] Dan O. Via and Amos N. Wilder were the most notable English-speaking authors of this period[5] and the journal *Semeia* contained many relevant articles. One really fortunate circumstance in France was that structuralists and biblical exegetes began at a very early stage to bring out joint publications and that structuralists also independently examined parts of the Bible (and are still doing this).[6] The very fact that there is no specifically 'structuralist' biblical journal is an indication of the integration of this form of research into the framework of biblical study.[7]

AN INTANGIBLE AND MANY-HEADED MONSTER

I am of the opinion that structuralism and the linguistic analysis of texts can be of great help in our study of Scripture and, like many other exegetes, I have tried to extend my methods of research by including structuralism. In this task, however, exegesis is confronted with a number of problems. What any exegete first tries to do here is to find a connection between the study of biblical texts and the general principles of contemporary linguistics and, on this basis, to form a justified theory. It soon becomes clear, however, that linguistic analysis is an intangible and many-headed monster and the exegete wonders whether he will ever be able to subdue it. Why is this task so difficult? Let me confine myself to a few points.

In the first place, like 'theology', linguistic analysis as such has no real independent existence. It is only when it is delineated over and against other disciplines that it is possible to speak about it in general terms. Anyone entering the linguistic building will quickly discover how many different approaches it accommodates. There are, of course, general introductions that reflect, at least to some degree, a consensus of opinion. It is, however, an illusion to think that one can gain a firm grasp of linguistics by reading, for example, J. Lyons' introduction to the subject.[8] It is true that the three levels of linguistics—phonology, grammar and semantics—are discussed in this book, especially in their interrelationship. But as soon as one begins to find one's way, one becomes aware of many differences of opinion. What is more, linguistics are more like a living being than a building, because the study is continuously developing and diversifying, to such an extent that it is difficult to seize hold of it. Indeed, it does resemble a slippery and many-headed monster and the exegete who is struggling with it is always afraid that what he is reading at a given moment may already be out of date.

Another problem is that there is a considerable difference between one author's terminology and another's. This complicates the study of linguistics. (It is, I think, significant that there are more lexicons and dictionaries of linguistics than of any other subject.) It is clear, then, that the use of linguistic terminology is surrounded by snares. It is only to a limited degree that one can be sure of using a generally accepted nomenclature. And even then, whether it is true or not, the exegete inevitably feels that he is an amateur in the field of linguistics and is permanently troubled by increasing uncertainty.

The exegete feels uncertain, moreover, most of all in the very sector that is most relevant to exegesis. He is naturally interested in the help that linguistics can give him in the interpretation of books and texts in the Bible. The classical works of linguistic analysis, however, go no further than grammatical sentences and the relatively few publications on linguistic expressions that transcend the scale of a sentence show even less consensus of opinion than the works of those authors who are concerned with the grammatical sentence, even if the terminology used is not (to give only two examples out of many) that of textual linguistics or generative poetics. And anyone who thinks that he will find a suitable interpretation of texts in semantics will inevitably be disappointed.

Finally, the exegete will soon be troubled by questions about the size of the monster with which he is locked in combat. Should, for example, the traditional study of literature, which is in many ways moving along a parallel course to that of linguistic analysis, be regarded as one of the branches of linguistics? What, too, should we think of semiotics? Language is clearly the most developed and most privileged system of signs that we have and semiotics, which are concerned with sign-systems, speak above all about language. Does this mean, then, that the exegete must include semiotics? He will in any case fear that he is caught in an expanding universe. Every time that the limits of the study come closer, they seem to be moving away again.

It is not a purely imaginary danger that the exegete will eventually be defeated and even swallowed by the monster of linguistics. In any case, it is certain that the exegete who tries to remove this uncertainty by reading more and more about linguistics will never come to an end of his study and may well forget his task as an exegete in the course of it.

Ought he, then, to seek safety in flight? It is clear to me that, if he runs away, he will cut himself off not only from a branch of science that is in itself very valuable, but also from a great deal that might be very useful to him in his own branch of learning. The only possibility that is open to him, then, is to try to subdue the monster, in other words, to make linguistics serviceable for exegetical work. He can do this best by using linguistics as an ancillary science alongside (or instead of—there is a difference of opinion about this) other sciences.

This is certainly not a simple task. I have already referred at the beginning of this article to a number of problems, such as the size of the territory, the speed of development in ideas, the diversity of views and the complexity of the terminology. These are all snares for the exegete who is following the trial of linguistics. One other trap, however, has to be mentioned in particular and that is the danger of an eclectic use of linguistics. There is, after all, a great temptation to be arbitrary in one's selection from the armoury of linguistics and only to choose those weapons that can be of immediate use and to leave the others where they are. If he does this, the exegete would be ignoring the fact that there is one single coherent whole of views in linguistics, in which all the levels of a linguistic expression are covered and interrelated. The alternative to an eclectic use of this kind is not, of course, to carry out all the processes that may occur in the linguistic model of research. A phonological analysis should, for instance, only be carried out if there is a good reason to do so on a basis of the text in question. The better alternative is for the exegete to master for himself the principles and points of departure of a linguistic model. It is only when he has done this and it is only within this framework that concrete operations can be carried out. And which operations should in fact be performed ought clearly not to be based on an arbitrary choice, but on the nature of the questions for which an answer has to be found and the relationship between the exegetical questions and the parts and levels of the linguistic analysis.

A BREAK WITH THE METHOD OF HISTORICAL CRITICISM?

To what extent does linguistic analysis of a biblical text represent a break with the method of historical criticism and especially with form criticism and the history of traditions? And, if there is in fact a break between the two, are the methods used in each case so different that they are mutually exclusive? What are these differences in attitude and method between the earlier exegesis using form criticism and the history of traditions and the newer linguistic exegesis? These are all questions that concern exegetes today in their choice of method and it is certain that not every exegete would answer them in the same way.

In France, exegetes have come to accept structuralism almost without difficulty as a method of analyzing biblical texts. A very interesting example of this easy transition is provided by two studies by Jean Delorme on the resurrection, the first presented in 1967 and the second in 1970. In the first, he studied the resurrection within the framework of historical criticism,[9] whereas, in the second, he used the linguistic approach.[10] It is striking in this context that Delorme did not mention explicitly at the two congresses any change in his methods or insights, nor did he in any way withdraw the earlier study at the second congress. This silent transition is a very remarkable illustration of the way in which the development has taken place in France.

The situation is quite different in Germany. Two books mark the beginning of this transition and there is no doubt that both authors believed that a clear break had taken place. W. Richter said explicitly that the concept of historical criticism could no longer be used in exegesis,[11] although he did not go so far as to claim that the diachronic aspects were no longer relevant.[12] E. Güttgemanns was even more polemical.[13] His publications led—in my view, wrongly—to a serious conflict and the eventual withdrawal of a subsidy for Güttgemanns' institution in Bonn.[14] This atmosphere of conflict is in striking contrast to the much more harmonious transition in France.

Whether or not there has been a real break depends, I think, at least partly on where the accent is placed. It is clear that form criticism and the history of traditions include elements that lend themselves to an extension of the linguistic method of analysis. Both these earlier approaches claim to base their conclusions on empirical data that are to a great extent found in the text of Scripture itself. Form criticism is also very much concerned with the structural elements of the smallest textual units and the history of traditions is similarly concerned with the editing of the final text. If this is where the accent is placed, then linguistically orientated exegesis may be seen as a continuation of exegesis based on historical criticism of the kind practised in the last twenty or so years. This is one way of avoiding a very important difference, which cannot really be overlooked.

This difference is found in the relevance of the word 'history' that is so important in the terms 'form criticism' (*Formgeschichte:* form history) and 'history of traditions' (or the history of the editing of the Bible). The method of historical criticism had, in an earlier phase of its application, devoted its main attention to the question of the historical character and conditioning of the text, whereas more attention was devoted, in the later phase of form criticism and the history of traditions, to the historical development of the text. In the case of form criticism, this historical concern was for the history of the origin of the smallest units of text; in the case of the history of traditions, it was for the final edition of the Bible or a particular book. This accounts for the great interest in the *Sitz im Leben,* in other words, in the situation in which a unit of text or a book of the Bible arose. It also accounts for the concentration on the way in which the final editor may have concentrated on selecting, ordering, filling in and changing the material in the book in question. Our study of the particular biblical book may be dominated to a great extent by its dependence (assumed by us) on the situation in which it originated and various previously given textual data. This approach is, after all, essentially alien to our contemporary linguistic theory and practice. This contrast between two quite different approaches can, I think, be best summarized by the two words 'diachronic' and 'synchronic'.

I have already discussed—in rather a brief way, I admit, but that is inevitable in this article—the meaning of these two words. Now something has to be said about the background. For our point of departure, we may say that it is, according to certain authors, better to ignore a diachronic study of a biblical text, because such an approach would—if it took place within the framework of form criticism and the history of traditions, as it no doubt would—proceed from unproved and unprovable hypotheses about the way in which the text in question originated and the situation in which it was first placed. Whether this is true or not—and I myself think that it is only partly true—I am of the opinion that other reasons may also play a part in this matter, even if we are not at all or only slightly conscious of them. One fairly trivial reason is that the model of research based on form criticism and the history of traditions is not used in any comparable science. The biblical scholar using this model gives a rather dated and isolated impression in interdisciplinary dialogue. There may, however, be other, deeper reasons. I can imagine, for example, that exegesis based on historical criticism may well be associated with a view of man and the world that is characterized by the importance attached to relationships of cause and effect and to the conviction that something can best be known by going back to its causes. The fact that a diachronic study of the language of the Bible would undoubtedly come off worse in comparison with a synchronic approach may well be connected with an increasingly sceptical attitude towards all models that are determined by the relationship between cause and effect.

ANOTHER ATTITUDE AND PROCEDURE

It is clear that an exegete who uses a more linguistically orientated method will have an attitude and a procedure that is different from that of an exegete who works with historical criticism. Let me mention here a number of these differences. I do this with some diffidence, since the steps that I have myself made on the way towards a linguistically based form of exegesis are so small that I can regard myself as no more than an amateur in this field.

In a study of a text based on historical criticism, the exegete looks in the first place for joins and uneven patches in the texture of a given passage that may be of help to him in distinguishing units of text that may have existed independently in tradition from their editorial adaptation. It is only later that he will examine the formally closed character and the structural elements of the smallest units of text and the work as a whole. In describing the specific meaning of the final version of the text, he will rely on those elements for which the final editor was, in his opinion, directly responsible, perhaps, for example, because he added them himself.

The way in which the linguistically-orientated exegete looks at the text is quite different. He does not, for instance, look for things that seem to be out of order in the text. On the contrary, he proceeds on the assumption that the text is a single fabric and that he can distinguish the weft and the woof and the themes woven into the material. The data have to be seen as fitting into each other and as closely related parts of a single whole structure. If there are any textual elements left over that he cannot explain, he continues to look until he discerns a structure in which these elements also have their special place and function.

If a text (or part of a text) has biblical or extrabiblical parallels, these are also approached in a different way by the exegete who works with historical criticism and the scholar who is orientated towards linguistics. The former questions the mutual relationship that may exist between the parallel biblical and extrabiblical texts, whereas the latter regards them as variants of the same structure and does not feel that it is necessary to look at the distinctive aspects of each. He prefers to see how each variant throws light on the other and to look closely at the structure that they have in common.

Data outside the text also play a different part. The exegete using the method of historical criticism is very interested in determining the place and time of origin of the text he is studying, because these help him to find a concrete situation that may throw light on the way in which the text may have functioned and on the meaning of the text. The scholar who makes use of linguistics, on the other hand, may also be interested in the place and time of origin of the text, but for entirely different reasons. He is interested because the text can be linked, if he has this information, with other texts of the same period and the code that he is using can be determined more satisfactorily.

THE RELIEF OF THE GUARD

Does the emergence of this linguistically orientated exegesis mean the end of exegesis based on historical criticism? This would no doubt be the case if the two methods were mutually exclusive or if the more recent form of exegesis were to make the earlier form superfluous. In my view, however, neither the one nor the other is true.

In the first place, they are not mutually exclusive. They would only exclude each other if they were in opposition to each other and they are not. There is in principle no objection to the practice of using both kinds of textual analysis, one after the other, for the same text. It is even possible to claim that they to some extent have different objects—synchronic analysis relates to the text as it is given and in relation to comparable texts of the same period, whereas diachronic analysis relates to the whole complex of processes and circumstances which were present and played a part in the emergence of the text. The two studies by J. Delorme which I mentioned earlier in this article were written with a fairly long interval between them and they were not both concerned with exactly the same textual datum, but they can together be regarded as an example of the possibility of investigating the same datum by both methods.

Secondly, the linguistic approach to the bliblical text has not, in my opinion at least, made the method of historical criticism superfluous. I am convinced that the linguistic approach is best confined to a particular type of problem. I cannot at present decide whether this limitation is a fundamental one or whether it is simply factual, because I have not yet gained a comprehensive view of the whole question. There is, however, at least one factual imitation in that the linguistic approach to the Bible is generally confined to statements about intratextual and intertextual aspects of a particular text of the Bible. The exegete using this method does not ask—or only very seldom asks—and hardly ever answers questions about the relationship between a text and extratextual data and questions about the possible function of a text in the process of communication between the writer and his readers. In my opinion, for instance, most of the narrative sections of the gospels cannot be read as fictional stories.[15] This inevitably raises the question of the value of these texts as reality.[16] This is, of course, quite an important question for the theologian. The question of the function that a story or a book of the Bible may have in the process of communication between the writer and his readers is also important for the interpretation of the text. If this type of question is left entirely out of account—and I have the impression that this is the case in the study of biblical texts based on structuralist principles and semiotics—it may be possible to make meaningful statements about the 'meaning' of the text, but not about the 'significance' that the text in question may acquire again and again.[17]

For the time being at least, I find exegesis based on historical criticism indispensable. I am, however, bound to add at once that linguistically orientated exegesis is equally indispensable, particularly because it has shown me quite clearly that exegetes have used the method of historical criticism to look for answers to many important questions, but have tended to overlook, in their use of this method, questions about the meaning of the text and the significance that could be attributed to it. It has also become clear to me why most ordinary readers of the Bible have found form criticism and the history of traditions so confusing. This form of exegesis has in recent years been used to distinguish different levels within the text studied. This was a useful application of the method and it made an important contribution to our understanding of the text, but it was above all a model of research. As a model for reading the Bible, it was, however, not valuable, because no one can read the Bible at different levels of the text and, what is more, no single text can be read in that way, even if it did develop at many different levels.

I am also bound to admit that I have so far not always found linguistic analysis reliable, especially in certain essential aspects of exegesis. The most essential aspect for me—a biblical exegete—is the interpretation itself of the biblical text. And it is precisely at this point of interpretation that I find myself in a vacuum. Interpretation of a biblical text is, after all: What does that text mean for people? This is clearly a question for the sub-discipline of linguistics known as pragmatics. But, as far as my so far limited knowledge of linguistics is concerned, pragmatics are almost exclusively concerned with the spoken language and with speakers and listeners, a sphere in which questions arise that are radically different from those that occur in the process of communication between the writer and his readers. In this way, then, I am deprived of the help that I need at the most decisive point of interpretation. But, who knows, I may in the future find precisely the publication on linguistics that I need to solve this problem. Or perhaps the work that I am seeking will soon be published.

Translated by David Smith

Notes

1. I am thinking here of the way in which the members of the Societas Hebraica of Amsterdam work. They place great emphasis on the unity of the Bible and the ideolecta of the biblical language.

2. R. Barthes et al., *Exégèse et herméneutique* (Paris, 1971); idem, *Analyse structurale et exégèse biblique* (Paris, 1971).

3. I do not regard L. Alonso Schökel's studies and the structural analysis of the kind practised by A. Vanhoye and his school as linguistically orientated research.

4. See especially E. Güttgemanns, *Offene Fragen zur Formgeschichte des Evangeliums* (Munich, 1970); idem, *Studia linguistica neotestamentica* (Munich, 1971); see also various numbers of *Linguistica Biblica,* which have detailed bibliographies.

5. D. O. Via, *The Parables* (Philadelphia, 1967); A. N. Wilder, *Early Chris-*

tian Rhetoric. The Language of the Gospel (London, 1964; 2nd ed., Cambridge, Mass., 1974).

6. See, for example, L. Marin, *Sémiotique de la passion* (Paris, 1970); C. Chabrol and L. Marin, *Le récit évangélique* (Paris, 1974).

7. There are publications in journals of a general interest such as *Langages* 22 (June 1971), which is entitled 'Sémiotique narrative: récits bibliques'.

8. J. Lyons, *Introduction to Theoretical Linguistics* (Cambridge, 1st ed., 1968).

9. J. Delorme, 'Résurrection et tombeau de Jésus', P. de Surgy et al., *La résurrection de Jésus et l'exégèse moderne* (Paris, 1969), pp. 105-51.

10. J. Delorme, 'La résurrection de Jésus dans le langage du nouveau testament', H. Cazelles et al., *Le langage de la foi dans l'écriture et dans le monde actuel* (Paris, 1972), pp. 101-82.

11. W. Richter, *Exegese als Literaturwissenschaft* (Göttingen, 1971), pp. 17-18.

12. Ibid., pp. 70-72.

13. See above, note 4.

14. See E. Güttgemanns' notes in *Linguistica Biblica* 27/28 (September 1973), pp. 41-44.

15. There are fictional stories in the quoted speech of the gospels. These contain signs that point clearly to the fictional aspect. (They occur especially at the beginning.) These signs are not found in the narrative parts of the gospels.

16. Among the important contributions to this question are those by E. Güttgemanns, ' "Text" and "Geschichte" als Grundkategorien der Generativen Poetik', *Linguistica Biblica* 11/12 (January, 1972), pp. 2–12; idem, 'Linguistische Analyse von Mk 16, 1–8', *op. cit.*, pp. 13–53. Space prevents me from discussing Güttgemanns' ideas here.

17. For the difference between 'meaning' and 'significance', see E. D. Hirsch, Jr., *The Aims of Interpretation* (Chicago, 1976), especially pp. 1-13 and 79-81.

Alfredo Fierro Bardají

Consciousness of Change and Questioning of Theology

THERE IS no validity in the idea that the participation of Christians in revolutionary movements of a liberating nature is sufficient to bring about a revolution in theology. The history of Christianity, particularly in the period that produced so many messianisms, extending from the eleventh to the eighteenth centuries, shows the opposite to be the case. Throughout this period there were a series of ephemeral and intermittent disturbances—bloodily repressed, but with sufficient continuity to constitute a tradition of subversive Christianity as an alternative and counterweight to the dominant ecclesial mode—produced by the exuberant eruption of messianic and millenarian movements, egalitarian and/or libertarian in nature, with a utopian longing for a society without hierarchies or lords, without power and without distinctions, holding goods completely in common.[1]

These movements were far from dumb—they used the word: the evangelical, biblical, Christian and—particularly if this adjective is reserved for theories produced from within the Church—the theological word. The evangelical and biblical rumbling of messianisms and chiliasms—or, more widespread still, of popular sects and heresies—contradicted the official Church teaching which stemmed from the cleresy (the magisterium, the universities, the monasteries), but did not go so far as to question the nature and legitimacy of the discourse that we now call theological. Although they gave it a different socio-political meaning and content, the theology of the millennium and popular heterodoxy still trusted the same sources and the same proceedings as ecclesiastical and academic theology. Heretics and inquisitors, messianic *iluminati* and hierarchs of the Church were both equally convinced that they possessed a supernatural knowledge based on certain revealed Scriptures and qualitatively different from any other sort of knowledge.

SOCIO-POLITICAL CHANGE AND ENLIGHTENED CONSCIOUSNESS

So it is not the present spread and growth of liberation movements among oppressed classes, peoples and groups, nor—at least not only—the militancy of Christians in these movements (Socialist and Communist Christians, believers enrolled in guerrilla movements in politically and economically colonized countries, in struggles for the emancipation of racial minorities 'gay Christians', etc.) that is today producing a radical questioning of the very possibility of speaking theologically. This questioning does not stem directly from the practice of Christians involved in confrontation with the imperialist or neo-capitalist establishment, or with any irrational, authoritarian form of repression, but rather from the consciousness of this practice now generally felt. The contemporary theologian finds his discourse displaced, dislocated and even basically exiled from a socio-political atmosphere that makes the very existence of his product problematical.

It is undoubtedly the depth of economic, political and cultural changes, and the radicalism of the practice designed to bring them about, that in the final analysis brings about this dislocation and exile, but it does so through a new consciousness of social change and of socially changing practice. This is an historical, enlightened and critical consciousness; and this is what distinguishes it from the millenarian revolutionary consciousness. *Historical:* it views natural and social reality as changeable, susceptible to transformation through the activity of man—and this in a progressive or process fashion, not through a dichotomic and instantaneous representation breaking any continuity between the before and after (e.g., between the original Golden Age and the later state of fall; or between a miserable present and a glorious apocalyptic tomorrow. *Enlightened:* it develops its own rationale through a scientific understanding of nature, man and society. *Critical:* it is capable of questioning everything, including itself and its practice, enquiring into its own conditions of possibility and legitimacy.

The enlightened and critical consciousness enquires into what went before and what comes after it and its products: representations, words, discourses, ideologies. It is concerned with enquiring into what precedes it, what allows it to come into being and brings it about: pre-conscious and pre-verbal reality; and also into what follows it and the effects it will produce: practices and modifications in reality made possible through consciousness and language. Kant, Marx, Nietzsche, Freud, linguistics, cultural anthropology and, finally, the social sciences have all encouraged it in this enquiry and influenced the means by which it carries it out.

It is here, in and through the mediation of critical understanding of historical change, that the crisis for theology, ultimately deriving from this change itself, becomes apparent.

Christian theology has viewed itself as a science or word stemming directly from a science or word of God, to be found principally in the Bible. Its basis was revelation. Of course theology enquired into its conditions of possibility, into what went before it and made it possible as discourse, but it had an all-embracing reply to this question: revelation, the word or action of God in history. The orientation of such a reply—as hardly needs saying—is totally unsatisfactory to modern critical questioning of conditions for production of a discourse or system of representation. In fact if this is to be satisfied, we have to enquire into the origin and genesis not only of theology but also of the biblical texts—and indeed, of the very idea of revelation or divine action within history.

Theology still considered itself self-sufficient in another sense: that of not needing anything outside itself in the realm of the word in order to fulfil entirely the requirements of its own significance and truth. It is true that the theological word has recently been seeking a realization, a putting into practice, the analysis and development of which corresponds to what was called moral theology. But the practice deriving from theological teaching was a corollary, not an essentially constitutive element of its truth and meaning. The traditional statement that theological truth contains practical imperatives is in fact far removed from contemporary critical procedure, which asks of any product of understanding—or language—what practice embodies it, considering this practice as a decisive criterion for verification of whether—and how—a discourse is significant or true.

This second element of the enlightened consciousness of historical change can possibly be assimilated by theology without any grave disturbance of its traditional identity. This would seem to be shown by the fact that most theologians today have accepted it without debate. But their acceptance of it taken to its final consequences will involve them in serious difficulties, as I propose to show.

VERIFICATION THROUGH PRACTICE

It is a commonplace of present-day theology that the meaning and truth of Christian principles has to be established, verified and proved in the practice of believers. This is the equivalent of accepting the criterion that a discourse and word become meaningful and true, not only through what they say in themselves, but above all, through the practical reality surrounding them.[2] The meaning and truth of not only theological reflection but also of the Gospel message have to be highlighted, proved and justified by what Christians in fact do. There are several 'theologies'—of liberation, of social change, of revolution, etc.—specifically concerned with the actual practice of liberation, revolution or change which they signal out as the touchstone of this meaning and truth. So far no problem.

The problems appear when today's practical theologies—whether of liberation or the political theology more characteristic of central Europe—are forced to be somewhat more specific and to produce a circumstantial development of the relationship to practice which they have stressed in principle in a general way. Theology lacks its own proper means for such a development. If it is to carry it out, it needs the intervention of practical, non-theological rationality: an *ethic,* to give it its traditional denomination.[3] The essential link that political theology and the theology of liberation claim with political and liberating praxis, if it is not to be a purely abstract link, has to be assured by a political or liberating ethic. So far, so good, but the content of this ethical or practical rationality, both in its tools of analysis and in the models of action resulting from these methods, is something alien to theology. It is an emancipatory and sometimes revolutionary social ethos in which Christians happen to be taking part, but not specifically as Christians; furthermore they often take part in the wake of an alien protagonism and an historical initiative in which they have not taken part. In fact, theologians recognize that there is no such thing as a specifically Christian, political or social practice (even if they then generally try to distinguish—with less than brilliant success—what a Christian contribution to common practice might be).

So the consideration of the practical consequences of its own reasoning involves theology in requirements that are difficult to reconcile. On one side it is required to produce its credentials in practice, displaying the meaning and truth of what it says in the material demonstration of what Christians do. On the other side, the practice on which its very verification depends does not stem from theological or evangelical principles, but from a rational analysis of social reality. The present-day theologies of praxis only partly satisfy the principle that their discourse (or theory) should be highlighted and validated in praxis, since the practice they invoke does not strictly correspond to the same theological reasoning they are trying to validate, but to extra-theological theory and analysis.

ANALYSIS OF PRODUCTS OF THE REASONING PROCESS

The most radical, critical threat to the theological process does not stem so much from the requirement that it should be verified in its practical consequences, as from an analysis of its antecedents and the conditions that produced it. Modern enlightened consciousness seeks the keys to the meaning of a reasoning process in what precedes it and makes it possible. Who is talking? What is he trying to say? What socially definable objective interests underlie his words? What framework or linguistic, economic, and cultural constrictions defines the possibility, identity, and practical necessity for a particular set of verbal products? These are decisive questions in understanding what a verbal discourse is really saying. Their systematic discussion and examination form the subject matter of the critique of ideologies.[4]

Theologians today hasten to declare that they take up the challenge of critique of ideologies, and willingly so; they recognize ideological elements in their own teaching and in that of the official Church; they hasten to distinguish between faith and ideology, in order to work out a formulation of faith free from ideology. This widely-expressed appropriation of the critique of ideology can, however, have two limitations in its application. The first is that the critical thread of analysis of ideology is restricted to ecclesiastical and theological teachings, while its application stops short of biblical and evangelical texts, which are generally considered untouchable.[5] The second is that the concept of ideology adopted by theologians usually refers only to the system of representations produced by the dominant classes, a system objectively directed to the consolidation and legitimization of their dominance. This means that the theological appropriation of the critique of ideologies usually leaves out of account both the constitutive documents of the Christian tradition and an overall consideration of the production of ideologies. This, besides examining their possible relationship with the interest of the dominant classes, also embraces any relationship with socio-economic interests in general, including those of oppressed classes and groups, and has the essential task of setting any claim to understanding and meaning in its historical context.

In present-day theology, recognizing the presence of ideological components in Christianity and the consequent attempts to de-ideologize faith, generally come to mean no more than the discovery that Christianity in the framework of modern capitalism had developed a rationale objectively legitimizing the exploitation worked by the bourgeoisie on the working classes. This has led to an attempt to re-formulate faith in a way consonant with the work of emancipating dominated classes and peoples, but the fact that the ideological element is also present in biblical texts is left out of consideration; in particular, no attention is paid to the decisive fact that the principal result of the critique of ideology—of every ideology, not only that which serves dominant groups—is a reduction of any pretension to universal and absolute truth, including that of statements like 'God saves Man' or 'Jesus is Lord'.

It is in the critical act of going back to the conditions that produced the Christian word—including the word of annunciation or good news, not only that of dogmatic or theological discourse—that theology loses all inherent support; it even loses the link, till now considered beyond question, with a revelation or word of God, since analysis designed precisely to uncover the material conditions that make a word possible and determine it can find no tangible trace of such a thing. The original Gospel is also relativized and separated from its old connection with divine revelation: the fact that it is the subversive account of a liberating and subversive praxis—that of Jesus—can lend it unexpected possibilities of establishing live links with the emancipatory purpose of the popular levels of society of all times, thereby redeeming Christianity from the accusation of being an impenitent accomplice of all classes in power; but it does not bring it any nearer to being a word of God, that is a type of production that transcends the material facts which ideological analysis can scrutinize. To say that the Christian faith consists precisely in recognizing this word of God in the material conditions of the Gospel, and beyond these, is still leaping into the dark, not now passing by on the other side but acting directly contrary to the constituent character of the enlightened consciousness in Western countries today. Such a leap, furthermore, precisely in its presumption of transcending the material conditions of ideological production, shows that it is being produced in a false consciousness, deceiving itself about itself; that is, it shows itself to be an ideology in one of the characteristics of ideology revealed by classical analysis, that of false consciousness. Of all forms of believing consciousness, religious or Christian, none is so ideological as that which presumes itself free from the scope of analysis of ideologies.

THE EPISTEMOLOGICAL BREAK

The present-day theologian has to opt for one or other of two sorts of theology which generally march together in a syncretic amalgam in theological writing, but which strictly speaking are incompatible one with another. One of these is limited to development, amplification, and systematization of the spontaneous or ingenuous languages of faith: those of profession of faith, preaching, catechesis and dogma.

Such a development does not deserve the name of science or theory, nor does it count as critical discourse (which, let us say at once in order to avoid misunderstanding, does not indicate that it is in any way inferior: poetry and the theatre are not 'inferior' to science; but here it is a question of pointing out not which theology is superior or inferior, but which constitutes a critical discourse and which does not). To qualify as, strictly speaking, a critical, scientific and theoretic system, theological discourse has to take upon itself, in overall reflection on itself and on the other languages and practices of Christianity, the material conditions—economic, political, and social—that produced the Christian phenomenon and the Christian word, and also the conditions that verify it or validate it in practice. This requirement is generally expressed in the formula that a theology is critical in so far as it can be defined as critical of theology,[6] but it could also be formulated by saying that theology only qualifies for the critical level by making an epistemological break[7] with all spontaneous religious forms of consciousness (and of word); and by breaking also with its own past as a discipline which it necessarily shows to be ideological.

Can this critical theology, breaking with traditional theology and with the early languages of faith, still be considered theology? Is there any limit to radicalization in its criticism of theology, even a relative limit in the sense that once it is passed, criticism is no longer theological but extra-theological? The reply to these questions depends on criteria referring to what should be understood as the identity of a discipline and whether criticism of a discipline is always carried out from within it. One can think of two contradictory examples here: criticism of philosophy can continue to be philosophical; but chemistry, on the other hand, can include a criticism of alchemy, but this does not make it alchemy.[8] With regard to the question of theology, what name it gives itself can perhaps be left to individual taste. If criticism of theology, epistemologically breaking with the traditional past, is still to be called 'theology', this is possibly quite correct, although it would certainly be less misleading to call it something else, so that it would not be theology, however critical, that took the place of itself, but another discipline succeeding it and replacing it—as chemistry succeeded alchemy—another non-theological discipline, which could perhaps be called 'the critical theory of Christianity', or something similar.[9] The decisive question, however, is that of its essence; and with regard to this, one has to say that faced with the traditional content of theology, of dogma, of catechesis, and even of the announcement of the good news itself, the exercise of critical rationality does not in itself have any limit to the areas it can cover. Going beyond merely nominal disputation, the situation of the 'theologian' today is that he finds himself without proper epistemological instruments—unless he still dogmatically presumes to base himself on a revelation in the positivist mode—and that he possesses no mode of reasoning or critical tools other than those common to the secular or social sciences and even to science in general. This does not mean that his discourse has to be purely critical or negative, but it does mean that it will break with everything that was understood in the past as sacred doctrine or theology.

Translated by Paul Burns

Notes

1. N. Cohn, *In Pursuit of the Millennium* (London, 1957); idem, *Heresies and Societies in Pre-Industiral Europe* (London, 1963).

2. This criterion is common to the Marxist theory of the primacy of practice and to such disparate epistemologies as pragmatism, logical empiricism and existentialist philosophy.

3. T. Rendtorff and J.B. Metz are both very clear on this mediation of ethics in their respective contributions to *Diskussion zur 'politischen Theologie'* (Mainz/Munich, 1969), pp. 217-18 and 280-83.

4. Apart from the now classic texts of Marx and Mannheim, cf. J. Gabel, *Idéologies* (Paris, 1974); L. Sebag, *Marxisme et structuralisme* (Paris, 1967); T. Herbert, 'Remarques pour une théorie générale des idéologies', in *Cahiers pour l'analyse* 9 (1968), pp. 74-92.

5. Hence the commotion provoked by F. Belo, *Lecture matérialiste de l'évangile de Marc* (Paris, 1974), which dared to submit the untouchable text to ideological analysis.

6. As Xhaufflaire, Oudenrijn and others state.

7. The need for this break in order to establish a scientific discourse has recently been championed and developed by P. Bourdieu, J. C. Chamboredon and J. C. Passeron, *Le métier du sociologue* (Paris, 1973).

8. The example adduced by Engels to refute the thesis that atheism is another form of religion: cf. the selection of texts from Marx and Engels, *Sur la religion* (Paris, 1960), p. 235.

9. In a similar situation, in the Age of Enlightenment, those thinkers who took up the thematic discourse of theology, but broke with its tradition, decided to call themselves 'neologians' rather than theologians.

Tiemo Rainer Peters

Doing Theology as a Political Prisoner: The Example of Dietrich Bonhoeffer

IF I bring Dietrich Bonhoeffer, a long recognized historical and theological figure, world famous as the author of *Letters and Papers from Prison*,[1] into the discussion about the right place to do theology, it is not to blunt the immediacy of the question with historical anecdote, but if possible to sharpen it on a paradigm case.

Bonhoeffer fascinated the postwar generation of theologians primarily by his theology, solidly based and at the same time visionary, always embarking on new and daring hypotheses. He was also a challenge: people tried to bring 'system' into the complexity of his work. Bonhoeffer's acceptance became a reconstruction of his theology in systematic form.[2]

The present generation seems to be interested less in Bonhoeffer's theological system than in the authenticity of his thought, i.e., in the constant unity between his life and his theology. They are impressed by the fact that this theology always grew out of a totally unmistakeable situation, not one it had sought out, but one which it accepted in an active and serious commitment to its time.[3] The use of Bonhoeffer in future is more likely to be a practical one.

'No knowledge can be separated from the situation in which it is acquired' (Bonhoeffer)

Bonhoeffer was always concerned with the practical basis of belief and theology. In addition to his university teaching he worked as a youth chaplain among the Berlin proletariat in Wedding. He became involved in ecumenical work and was a key figure in resistance within the Church to the Nazis. He regarded Gandhi's satyagraha campaign of non-violent resistance as a model for Christian activity in the future. When he was deprived of his official authorization to teach in 1936, he had already cut his links with university theology, which was nevertheless indebted to him for many key ideas.

The idea of discipleship, which preoccupied Bonhoeffer after 1933 and which he developed in his Finkenwalde lectures between 1935 and 1937,[4] shows that Bonhoeffer understood the importance of practical activity as the theological problem par excellence. The central thesis of the book, 'Only the believer is obedient; only the obedient person is a believer' (p. 35), can be regarded as the first step towards a hermeneutics of practical theology.

In 1940 active commitment to his time and a faith which could not be silent drove Bonhoeffer into conspiratorial activity. His arrest in 1943 shows how high the price can be if theology and biography are to remain united. In *The Cost of Discipleship* Bonhoeffer had written, 'In a world which has become totally anti-Christian . . . the Christian is left only with the choice between flight from the world or imprisonment.'

Because Bonhoeffer's arrest (he rejected the idea of flight) is part of the logic, not just of his politics, but also, and above all, of his theology, prison could not destroy *this* theological existence. Quite the reverse, it challenged it to extremes of concentration. The cell in Berlin's Tegel prison became a radical site for the practice of theology.

Much of Bonhoeffer's argument in his letters from prison looks at first sight intelligible without reference to its place of origin. It continues almost undisturbed, without even signs of strain, putting forward many lavishly optimistic views which were nowhere else to be heard with such theological firmness. The ability to wrest this freedom from imprisonment is not just a sign of the underlying attitude of a Christian aristocrat which won Bonhoeffer the respect of his fellow prisoners. Ultimately it can only be understood as the result of a unique dialectical transformation. The culminating point of violence, the point at which, as it were, the massiveness of the Third Reich's contempt for humanity could be felt in its entirety, seems to have become the point of release for that liberating imagination and political and theological 'sense of the possible' which enabled Bonhoeffer to look forward to a future society 'come of age' and a new 'redeeming' Church.

This account in individual theological terms must, of course, not obscure a process which had general theological causes. As Hitler's Germany collapsed a new society was taking shape, pushing its way out of the web of political, economic and ethical compromises, involvements and complicities which had led to Nazi fascism.[5] Neverthe-less in Bonhoeffer this historical tendency was articulated in a language which possessed sufficient mystical depth not immediately to hand over the new possibilities to the routine of political or ecclesiastical prag-matists. His language revealed values ('true secularity', 'profound this-worldliness', 'pluridimensionality', 'the wager for others', 'suffer-ing with') which are permanently concealed by official social 'progress' in both east and west, and this indicates, in spite of all Bonhoeffer's resolute optimism, the underlying critical purpose of his theology. It is a product of a new association of theology and politics in which the old division of labour no longer obtains, one which was born in imprison-ment and becomes a model for us. We, the future generation, must not return, forgetful and untransformed, to the routine preoccupations of Church theology, or to the preoccupations of a trivial abstract maturity 'of the enlightened, the busy, the comfortable' (LPP, p. 369).

THE VIEW FROM BELOW

'There remains an experience of incomparable value. We have for once learnt to see the great events of world history from below, from the perspective of the outcast, the suspects, the maltreated, the power-less, the oppressed, the reviled.'[6] Bonhoeffer wrote that in 1942/1943 for his fellow conspirators. In the prison letters this 'view from below' attains a genuinely theological dimension, with consequences for her-meneutics, Christology and ecclesiology.

This practical hermeneutics, which first appeared in *The Cost of Discipleship,* now becomes central. The prisoner realizes why a change is necessary in the understanding of the relation between theory and practice: 'We have spent too much time in thinking, supposing that if we weigh in advance the possibilities of any action, it will happen automatically. We have learnt, rather too late, that action comes, not from thought, but from a readiness for responsibility. For your thought and action will enter on a new relationship: your thinking will be con-fined to your responsibilities in action. With us thought was often the luxury of the onlooker; with you it will be entirely subordinated to action' (LPP, p. 298). Part of what Bonhoeffer means is this: theology will only be able to preserve its identity if it gives up its position as onlooker and rigorously practises the view from below, if it recognises the primacy of committed action over theoretical contemplation 'from above'.

In Bonhoeffer's theology, the main implication of the view from below, sharpened as it was by imprisonment, is for Christology: 'That God draws near precisely where human beings usually turn away . . . is something that a prisoner can appreciate better than anyone else, and for him it really is good news, and by believing it he feels himself planted in the community of Christianity which bursts through all spatial and temporal barriers, and prison walls lose their meaning.'

The crucial figure here is the God who shares our suffering, understood not in terms of a reductionist, speculative *theologia crucis* but as part of a practical Christology, which, as it were, contains the redemptive idea of the resurrection in the practice of discipleship. 'Man is summoned to share in God's sufferings at the hands of a godless world' (LPP, p. 395). '. . . if we want to be Christians, we must have some share in Christ's large-heartedness by acting with responsibility . . . and by showing a real sympathy that springs, not from fear, but from the liberating and redeeming love of Christ for all who suffer' (LPP, 14).

This Christo-pathy is the late Bonhoeffer's real theological message, one which was formed in the political resistance and hardened in prison. It is not irrevocably fixated on suffering. Far from it. That would be 'an unhealthy methodism which deprives suffering of its element of contingency' (LPP, p. 374). The view from below reveals reality as its exists, stripped of its idealizations and ideological distortions, but it reveals it all the more clearly as distorted by suffering, both then and now, though this is something which is recognized more intensely in prison than in other places. The suspicion that imprisonment falsifies perception and so distorted Bonhoeffer's view is obviously a defensive reaction. It would be at least equally appropriate to be suspicious of the socially established, economically secure places where theology is practised, and of the 'orthodoxy' and 'balance' which usually prevails in them.

The view from below, which was the prevailing attitude in prison, leads Bonhoeffer finally to new ecclesiological insights. 'The Church is the Church only when it exists for others, not in a protective or populist attitude, but in radical 'participation'. 'Participation' seems to have had an irresistable hold on Bonhoeffer the political prisoner as the new word for 'discipleship': 'participation in the fate of Germany', 'participation in the sufferings of God in the secular life' (LPP, p. 361). The Church too has to participate 'in the secular problems of ordinary human life, not dominating, but helping and serving', giving up privilege and property: 'To make a start, it should give away all its property to those in need. The clergy must . . . possibly engage in some secular calling.'

It is clear that theology and the Church, if they were really to adopt this basis, would speak a new language and live in a totally different way. Bonhoeffer calls the new language of faith 'non-religious', and the related Christianity is 'religionless Christianity'. The premises of this paradoxically ecclesiological hypothesis of religionless Christianity can be given no more than a tentative formulation. Probably it was only prison which made it possible really to see through conventions and traditions, all the more when they had compromised themselves in the Third Reich. For this prisoner, who thought theologically and was used to thinking in alternatives, this opportunity bore fruit. In sum, Bonhoeffer saw that religion as a sublime metaphysical force, the essence of another order, of a dual morality, of flight from the world, interiority, individualism and the rest, had been a historical failure and (this is the prognosis he combined with the historical survey) no longer had any basis in the society of the future.[7]

This attack is directed primarily at bourgeois religion and its divisions of labour which lead to passivity, and the new basis for the Church and theology which is envisaged is one which is no longer defined exclusively by the bourgeoisie. This at least is the implication of the disappointed criticism of the theology of revelation (represented by Karl Barth and the Confessing Church). In Bonhoeffer's view it can be summed up as 'in the last analysis . . . essentially a restoration. For the religionless working man (or any other man) nothing decisive is gained here' (LPP, p. 280). 'Sociologically: no effect on the masses—an interest confined to the upper and lower middle class' (LPP, p. 381).

THE THEOLOGICAL CHALLENGE OF THE POLITICAL PRISONER

Theologians have been keen to separate Bonhoeffer's prison theology from the political prisoner Bonhoeffer. The prisoner Bonhoeffer was long regarded, and is to some extent still regarded, as an enthusiast, a traitor, the organizer of an 'unpatriotic' conspiracy.[8] Consciously or unconsciously, the prisoner was kept safely stoppered, and the prison theology was distilled off, abstract and unreal. Bonhoeffer's theology was transported away from the radical place of imprisonment back to the privileged places where theology is normally practised, back to the universities and the studies of systematicians of all sorts.

This is not to deny that important research was done in these places. Nevertheless Bonhoeffer's prison theology will only be fruitful in the long run if the place of its origin is not trivialized or neutralized, and when the allegedly romantic radicalism of the resistance fighter is taken seriously as a theological statement. Where this is forgotten Bonhoeffer is forgotten.

And for the same reason the place where this theology is developed is where it allies itself, or feels allied with the Christian and non-Christian resistance fighters opposed to the lack of freedom, injustice, cynical power and contempt for human beings in the world.[9] Theology is dangerous when it tries to remain true to its profession in the face of the bourgeois division of labour which separates religion from society and spirituality from solidarity. This is the challenging truth which Bonhoeffer confirmed in the radical theological place, the place of imprisonment and murder, in Tegel and in the Flossenburg concentration camp—a model for an uncompromisingly committed Christianity.

Translated by Francis McDonagh

Notes

1. 3rd revised and enlarged edition, London, 1967 and 1971. This edition supersedes the previous English collections. Abbreviated: LPP.

2. There is a comprehensive systematic account in E. Feil, *Die Theologie Dietrich Bonhoeffers* (Munich and Mainz, 2nd ed., 1971).

3. This new view was made possible largely by E. Bethge's great Bonhoeffer biography, *Dietrich Bonhoeffer. Theologe—Christ—Zeitgenosse* (Munich, 1967); (E.T. *Dietrich Bonhoeffer, Theologian, Christian Contemporary,* London, 1970). For an attempt at a theological-biographical interpretation of Bonhoeffer, cf. T. R. Peters, *Die Präsenz des politischen in der Theologie Dietrich Bonhoeffers* (Munich and Mainz, 1976).

4. D. Bonhoeffer, *Nachfolge* (Munich, 1937) (E.T., *The Cost of Discipleship,* London, 1952).

5. Cf. on this the still illuminating analyses of H. Müller, *Von der Kirche zur Welt* (Leipzig, 2nd ed., 1966).

6. D. Bonhoeffer, *Gesammelte Schriften,* ed. E. Bethge, vol. II (Munich, 2nd ed., 1965).

7. The fact that Bonhoeffer's prognosis was so clearly wrong is a criticism not of him, but of a Church and theology which think they can acquire a new identity on the back of a 'religious wave' which has no specifically Christian features.

8. On the relevance of this view, cf. E. Bethge, 'Protokoll einer Verhandlung', *Evangelischer Kommentar* 9 (1976), pp. 618ff.

9. Cf. on this C. A. L. Christo, *Brasilianische Passion. Die Briefe des Pater Betto aus dem Gefängnis* (Munich, 1973); J. de Santa Ana, 'Der Einfluss Bonhoeffers auf die Theologie der Befreiung', in: H. Pfeifer, ed., *Genf '76. Ein Bonhoeffer-Symposion* (Munich, 1976), pp. 151-63.

Fumio Tabuchi

The Theologian in Prison: Kim Chi Ha

PATRIOTIC POET AND REVOLUTIONARY

FRANCIS KIM CHI HA, whose civil name is Kim Young Il, was born
on 4 February 1941 in Mokpo, South Korea. He began his studies at the
State University of Seoul in 1959, but interrupted them two years later
and travelled around his country. Soon after he had returned to the
university, he was imprisoned because he had taken part in the students' resistance movement against the so-called Korean-Japanese
Normalization negotiations. In prison, he was also tortured. This did
not prevent him from energetically opposing a new economic
hegemony of the erstwhile colonial lords of Japan when he was released from prison. This was in 1965.

When he had finished his studies in aesthetics, he worked for a time
at various trades and professions (including that of a miner). It was
during this period that he began to write. It was also during this period
that his tubercular condition worsened and he was compelled in 1967 to
spend a long time in the TB Sanitorium of Masan. After his discharge in
1969, he worked on film scripts, dramas and poetry. In May 1970, his
satirical poem 'Five Bandits' (O Chok)[1] was published in the intellectual magazine *Sasangge* ('The World of Ideas'). This poem later became one of his best-known works. It was so positively received that it
was reprinted in the organ of the New Democratic Party of the opposition, *Minju Chonson* ('Democratic Front'). This journal was seized by
the South Korean secret service (KCIA) and the author and the publishers and editors of both magazines were imprisoned and accused of
an offence against the anti-communist law. As, however, there is no
instruction in the law in question under which the matter could be
subsumed, the accused were released in September 1970 when legal

84

proceedings were suspended. A declaration made by members of the International Conference of the PEN Club, which was being held in Seoul at that time, and various international protests tipped the balance in Kim's favour, so that he was released on bail after only a few months' detention. Kim's experiences of suffering at this time led to his conversion to Catholic Christianity and he was baptized in the spring of 1971.

Three months later, he published his first anthology Hwang-To ('Yellow Earth'). In an effort to avoid further accusations because of his political activities, he lived in the country and wrote prose and verse. The performance of one of his plays was, however, forbidden. In December 1971, a Japanese anthology of his poetry was published ('The Long Darkness'). In 1972, he published, in the Catholic journal Chang-Jo ('Creation', April edition), his second and longer satire 'Groundless Rumours' (Bi-O),[2] a bitterly ironical criticism of South Korean society. All the copies of this number of the journal were at once seized by the KCIA and the publisher and chief editor were tried. After a search lasting a few months, Kim was tracked down and once again arrested. He was cross-examined and tortured for two weeks and then, against his will, he was sent to the TB Sanitorium and kept there under arrest in a cell, despite his serious illness. By threatening him and his friends and relatives, the KCIA tried to prevent him from contacting the foreign press. At the same time, an 'arrangement' was suggested to him—he would be released, he was told, if he ceased to criticize the government. In the future, if he accepted the terms of this arrangement, he was to write more anti-communist works. Kim is reputed to have replied to this suggestion that he would rather give up his activity as a writer than satisfy this demand.

He was officially accused on 31 May 1972. The public prosecutor regarded Kim's direct attack against the government and public justice in his satire 'Groundless Rumours' as much more dangerous than his criticism in 'Five Bandits' and accused him, under the anti-communist law, of favouring the North Korean communists and of defaming the South Korean government. An international campaign, centred in Japan, was launched to secure the poet's release. A delegation of Japanese writers visited the Prime Minister of South Korea in Seoul and presented him with a petition. The members of the delegation were allowed to see Kim in Masan and on 18 July he was released from detention in the sanatorium.

His re-arrest and return to the TB Sanatorium of Masan at the end of 1972 therefore came as something of a surprise. At the beginning of December of that year, the case against the publication of his poem 'Five Bandits' was opened once again. There were worldwide protests and these led to his release in the spring of 1973. He was married in the April of that year.

A poem entitled 'Cry of the People'[3] that appeared after the demonstrations that took place on 3 April 1974 was the work of Kim Chi Ha and on 25 April he was once again in prison. This time he was accused of having given support to the National Democratic League of Youth and Students that had been banned by a special emergency decree (No. 4) and of having promised money to this league. On 13 July he was, together with six other accused, condemned to death, but this sentence was commuted a week later to life imprisonment. On 15 February[4] 1975, he was released on suspension of the penalty.

At the end of that month, he published an account of his ten months' imprisonment in Seoul entitled 'The Way of Suffering 1974'.[5] At the beginning of August 1975, Kim's 'Declaration of Conscience'[6] which was some twelve thousand words in length was smuggled out of prison and published in Tokyo. Shortly before then, the Park régime had tried, with the help of a good deal of intrigue, to brand the people's poet as a 'cunning and evil demagogue' and he had been arrested for the fifth time. In June 1975, the Afro-Asiatic authors' conference had passed a resolution to award the special Lotus Prize to Kim.

Kim's 'Declaration of Conscience' was recognized as authentic by Cardinal Kim Sou Hwan, the Archbishop of Seoul, the family of the poet and the Japanese Justice and Peace Commission and it was distributed by the latter organization. In this declaration, Kim stressed that the conspirators of the Park régime were plotting not only against him as an individual, but also against all those who were working to restore democracy to South Korea and against the Churches, because they had taken up the fight for social justice.[7] He also rejected the confession that he had been compelled to sign.[8] The National Christian Council of Japan in 1975 and the Catholic Commission for Justice and Peace in 1976 organized worldwide protests on behalf of Kim and against the Park régime and were joined in this activity by many theologians, including J. Cone, Harvey Cox, H. Gollwitzer, H. E. Tödt, Karl Rahner and Johann Baptist Metz, who also added their signatures.

In December 1976, Kim Chi Ha was condemned, not to death but to seven years hard labour on a charge of violating the anti-communist law. If the president's emergency regulations are rescinded in the near future, only penal servitude for life would be annulled; Kim is serving a sentence with hard labour on the charge of violating the regulation forbidding all criticism of the Yushin constitution that has been valid since 27 December 1972 (No. 1) and the regulation banning the National Democratic League of Youth and Students (No. 4; under threat of the death penalty). Kim's sentence of seven years' imprisonment would seem to have been a trick to ensure that he would remain in prison. He is kept in a solitary cell, 4.2 square meters in size, and under constant observation by television camera. In the winter of 1976-1977, his satire 'Jesus with the Golden Crown' (the Seoul Threepenny Opera) was performed as a Brecht-type musical.

PEOPLE'S THEOLOGIAN AND POLITICAL MYSTIC

Kim Chi Ha's 'Declaration of Conscience' represents the highest point of his work. In it, he has written a history of the life and ideas of a sincere Christian who is looking forward, in prison, to the free and democratic kingdom of God that is to come. His life-story is enacted within the framework of restricted information, ideological prejudice and lack of freedom.

Although (or perhaps because?) he has never in fact studied theology as a discipline, the writings of this lay convert to Christianity are marked by a deep theological and philosophical insight and perspicacity. In this sense, Kim can certainly be called a 'theologian', since anyone who speaks sincerely about God is a theologian in the wider and essentially true sense of the term.

In his most recent trial, he declared: 'As I have said again and again, my way of thinking is not so mature or systematic that it can be given a name. If, however, it has to have a name, then it could be called a philosophy of unity. My philosophy is an attempt to explain and overcome contradiction by creating a world of friendship and unity. For a very long time I have dreamed of the union of God and revolution, bread and freedom, heaven and earth, prayer and action. This philosophy has arisen from my own personal experience—I come from the people—from my life as a poet and from my religious faith. I believe that this philosophy that I follow is the need of our generation and our people. The urgent problem of the Korean people today is the union of north and south. But this is not simply a problem of territorial reunion. The authentic union of the people themselves is the basis of my philosophy. It is only through unity that our people can live, overcome oppression both inside and outside our country and help the world to achieve genuine brotherhood. This unity cannot be achieved either by compromise and strategy or by force. What is needed is an entirely new philosophy, an entirely new spirituality and an entirely new humanity. I cry out for this like a madman in this court. The ultimate aim of this philosophy is the state that Christians call *koinonia*. But the immediate problem with which we have to fight here and now is how to produce a national democratic revolution in our present situation . . .'[9]

According to Kim Chi Ha, Christianity is a revolutionary religion in the widest sense of the word. In the Bible, there are many places in which the exploiting, powerful people are thrown down and the insignificant, poor and oppressed people are accepted, set free, comforted and raised up. This is revolutionary thinking. In the widest sense, however, Christian revolution points to an apocalyptic vision of the rising up of peoples. In a permanent interrelationship of shared struggle and shared prayer, this uprising creates a space of hope for those who mourn, makes active brotherly love a reality and, by bringing about the kingdom of God on earth, fulfils a never-ending expectation.

In the Old Testament, Yahweh intervened in the history of man and put an end to injustice. He pointed again and again through his prophets to the way to justice and peace. In the New Testament, certain ways to justice and peace are indicated. These include a denial and a sacrifice of self, love of one's fellow-men and a dissociation from unjust commitments and pleasures.

The main aim of the theology of liberation is to point out these revolutionary principles in the contemporary political situation and to let them be seen as the Christian's sphere of action.[10] The leading exponent of a political theology, Johann Baptist Metz, has stressed that the eschatological promises of the biblical tradition—freedom, peace, justice and reconciliation—cannot be 'privatized', but force us again and again to be socially responsible.[11]

Elsewhere, Metz has argued that Jesus' message was essentially political in that it proclaimed the dignity of the human person and the state of all men as subjects in the presence of God. Those who bear witness to the gospel have therefore to champion the cause of man as a subject wherever that status is threatened. Christians have the task, Metz has emphasized, of ensuring that men continue to be subjects despite increasing collective coercion and that they can become subjects by emerging from misery and oppression. This task is, according to Metz, one of the most urgent imposed on us by the evangelical counsel of poverty.[12]

In Kim Chi Ha's poetry, many concepts lose their customary ideologically tinged meanings and are filled with an entirely new content. 'Revolution', for example, becomes the 'mystery of the resurrection' and is made a reality 'by man's religious decision and his inner spiritual rebirth'.[13] 'Violence' becomes the 'violence of love', 'not the violence that destroys humanity, but the violence that wins it back'.[14] He makes use in this way of certain politically stimulating words—in the same way that they are used so frequently in Latin America—to express his own faith and the promptings of his conscience. 'The heart of my drama is Christian eschatology', he said once and in this way expressed his opposition to the tabu surrounding such words as 're-volution', 'freedom' and 'bourgeoisie'. 'Why should I call a flower anything but a flower,' he exclaimed, 'because Marx happened to have called a flower a flower?'[15] Again, in his 'Declaration of Conscience', he insisted: 'What has always concerned me has been the unity of the principles of social reform as expressed in Marxist principles and the Christian principles expressed, for example, in the "Declaration of Santiago 1972" '.[16]

A little further on in the same text, he says: 'I find the idea of the unity between God and revolution elucidated by the mystery of the bread of Jesus that points, in the earthly form of a miracle, to the future life beyond this earth. This was stressed by Pope John XXIII in his *Mater et Magistra*. The same idea has been given an even more con-crete expression in the writings of modern theologians of liberation (J. Cone, R. Shaull, P. Lehmann, J. Moltmann, J. B. Metz, H. E. Tödt, H. Assmann, R. Niebuhr, D. Bonhoeffer and others) and in the papal documents that have appeared since the Second Vatican Council and such earlier texts as *Rerum Novarum* and *Quadragesimo Anno*. More than anything else, however, my own participation in the civil rights movement that has been promoted with great energy by the Korean Church since 1972 has convinced me that, in the conditions that prevail in a country so full of contradictions as Korea, unwavering resistance and a popular tradition of revolution are the materials from which a new principle of human liberation, the principle of the unity of God and revolution, can be forged. I am inclined to predict that this rich seam of gold that is deep inside the Korean earth will provide the world—and especially the Third World—with a very important message. If this material is carefully fashioned by the theology of liberation, God's mission will certainly produce a miracle of an entirely new shape from the simple tradition of struggle among the Korean people'.[17]

Kim Chi Ha has tried, in his so far unpublished ballad 'Chang Il Tam', to express this theme in the style of the Gospel by following the spiritual quest and the teaching of a religious man. The Park régime said that the author of this modern fable had committed the 'crime of writing texts hostile to the state'. The author himself, on the other hand, has said quite different things about his fable. According to Kim, it describes a still imperfect world in which various themes are strug-gling with each other in a turbulent whirlwind. These themes include religious ascesis and revolutionary action, the activity of Jesus and the struggle of Choi Su Woon and Jeun Bong Jun (the leader of the Tong Hak revolution), longing for the community life of the early Christians, participation in the unrelenting resistance movement of the Korean people, Paulo Freire's ideas about the education of the suppressed peoples, Frantz Fanon's theory of violence, the radicalism of Blanqui, the Christian teaching about original sin, the Catholic doctrine of the omnipresence of God, the popular activism of Lim Gok Chung[18] and Hong Kil Dong[19] and Tong Hak's idea of waiting for God and taking care of God.[20]

Let me conclude with a quotation from Kim Chi Ha's 'Way of Suffering 1974': '. . . every second in this cell was death. Confrontation with death! Should one be victorious in this confrontation and find the inner freedom of the fighter or should one submit in shame to defeat? The whole year of 1974 was, in a word, death and the name of our cause was: the struggle with death. The way of suffering was the mystery of the cross, that death should be overcome by deciding to die. That was our task'.[21] This quotation shows that Kim Chi Ha can rightly be called a mystic. 'The word of God is not fettered' (2 Tim 2.9).

Translated by David Smith

Notes

1. Kim Chi Ha, *Five Bandits: Cry of the People and Other Poems* (Hayama, Japan, 1974), pp. 39-59.

2. Ibid., 'Groundless Rumours', pp. 60-89.

3. Ibid., 'Cry of the People', pp. 90-111.

4. This is by pure chance the same date as that of the death of Camilo Torres, who died in 1966 in the fight for the liberation of Colombia. Kim Chi Ha shows in his 'Declaration of Conscience' (see below) how much he valued this coincidence.

5. Kim Chi Ha, *Kim Chi Ha* (Tübingen, Munich and Hamburg, 1976), pp. 13-33. This brochure was published as material for action by the Forum for Democracy in Korea (Tübingen) with a foreword provided by the publishers. The Munich edition (published by the Missio Internationales Katholisches Missionswerk) and the Hamburg edition (published by the Evangelische Arbeitsgemeinschaft für Weltmission) have different forewords. In all three editions, however, the reader will find 'Who is Kim Chi Ha?' ('Wer ist Kim Chi Ha?'), 'The Way of Suffering 1974' ('Leidensweg . . . 1974'), 'Letter to the priests' ('Brief an die Priester') and 'Declaration of Conscience' ('Gewissenserklärung').

6. Ibid., pp. 34-103; see also L. Kaufmann, 'Das Bekenntnis des Dichters Kim Chi Ha', *Orientierung* 39 (1975), p. 177; H. H. Sunoo, 'The Story of Kim Chi Ha', *Worldview* (June 1976), pp. 18-22.

7. Kim Chi Ha, 'Brief an die Pfarrer der "Nationalen Vereinigung der katholischen Priester für die Verwirklichung der Gerechtigkeit" ', in *Kim Chi*

Ha, pp. 8-12; The Emergency Christian Conference on Korean Problems, ed., *The Documents on the Struggle for Democracy in Korea* (Tokyo, 1975); Pressestelle im Sekretariat der Deutschen Bischofskonferenz, ed., *Christen unter dem Kreuz* (Bonn, 1976), pp. 45-47; W. Hunger, 'Kirchenkampf in Südkorea?', *Die katholischen Missionen* 96 (1977), pp. 55-59.

8. See also Kim Chi Ha, *Kim Chi Ha*, pp. 34-36 (Section 1: 'Bin ich ein Kommunist?', pp. 37-46; Section 4: 'Verletzte ich das Antikommunismus-Gesetz?', pp. 73-84).

9. An extract from Kim Chi Ha's final statement to the court on 23 December 1976, taken from an information script in Japan (the whole statement lasted more than three hours); this script is entitled *Kim Chi Ha's Philosophy of Unification (An Abridgement of Kim Chi Ha's Final Statement in Court, December 23, 1976)* and was published by the Japanese Catholic Council for Justice and Peace.

10. For Kim's view of revolution and violence, see his 'Declaration of Conscience', Section 2: 'Über Demokratie, Revolution und Gewalt', in *Kim Chi Ha*, pp. 46-58; ibid., Section 5: 'An alle, die Freiheit und Gerechtigkeit lieben', pp. 85-88; see also 'Kim Chi Ha im Kreuzverhör', *Orientierung* 40 (1976), pp. 177-79; 'Report on Kim Chi Ha's Trial Session, September 1976', *Interflow* (March-April, 1977), pp. 6-9; J. H. T. Lee, 'My Impressions concerning Kim Chi Ha's Memos written in Confinement', *Interflow* (March-April, 1977), pp. 9-13.

11. J. B. Metz, *Zur Theologie der Welt* (Mainz and Munich, 1968), p. 105.

12. Idem, *Followers of Christ. The Religious Life and the Church* (London and New York, 1978), especially pp. 47-59.

13. See Kim Chi Ha, 'Declaration of Conscience', especially Section 3: 'Einer revolutionären Religion entgegenräumend—die Welt von Chang Il Tam', pp. 58-72, especially p. 61.

14. Ibid., p. 54.

15. Ibid., p. 77.

16. Ibid., p. 62. The 'Declaration of Santiago 1972' mentioned in this quotation is the concluding document of the conference on 'Christians for Socialism' held in April 1971 in Santiago in Chile. It called for the synthesis of Christian faith and revolutionary commitment. See *Primer Documento de Trabajo: Cristianos por el Socialismo. Primer Encuentro Latinoamericano. Texto de la Edición Internacional* (Santiago, 1972).

17. Kim Chi Ha, *Kim Chi Ha*, pp. 64-66.

18. Korea's Robin Hood.

19. Hong Kil Dong is the main character in a novel by Ho Kyun, who was condemned on a charge of treason in 1617. Hong Kil Dong was the son of a high-ranking official who rebelled and became a bandit. He was the leader of the 'Let the Poor People Live' Party, which aimed to set up a paradise for the poor.

20. Inspired by Tong Kak's teaching, the Tong Hak peasant war (1894-1895) was waged. This was the beginning of the national liberation movement in Korea.

21. Kim Chi Ha, *Kim Chi Ha*, p. 18.

William Dwyer

The Theologian in the Ashram

GENERAL CONTEXT

THERE IS a good deal of introspection in the Church in India these days. One finds a concern for, and some reorientation in, the life of the Church, and many, young and old, bishops, priests and laity are having a tough passage into the new Church as envisaged at the second Vatican Council, or as spoken of, for instance, by Paul VI ten years afterwards in *Evangelii Nuntiandi*. The pain of this new growth is nowhere more vividly exemplified than in the transition many priests have had to make from the theology taught and studied in preparation for their pastoral ministry, to the actual theologizing and pastoral work encumbent on them now. It could be that they were taught theology and not to theologize, but that is another question. And if it is true that the courses and text-books of scholastic philosophy and theology (in Latin for the most part) have proved inadequate even for the future priests of the West, how much more lamentably inadequate and irrelevant do they now appear for the training of priests in a country like India.

The ministry and mission of the Church in Europe from Trent to Vatican II could not have been more antipodean from the task of the Church in India during the same period, but theology took little notice of this. Ricci and de Nobili were all too short-lived flowers in a field which remained barren until the early decades of this century. The Calcutta Jesuits under the influence of Pierre Charles, and Frederic Lebbe in China, were the first stirrings of a new approach to the mission of the Church.

India is after all unique in the history of the mission of the Church. Pre-Christian Israel had its own theology and devotional literature which to a large extent became the portion of the early Church.

Greece, Rome, Egypt, Asia Minor, and barbarian Europe, however, had religions and deities in plenty, but no theology or devotional heritage comparable to that of Israel. China and Japan came to constitute unprecedented cases in the history of the expanding Church. But above all, India. Christianity's entry into India, whether in the first century, the sixteenth or the twentieth, was an unprecedented encounter with a highly religious culture of great antiquity, replete with theologies, philosophies, devotional practices, monasticism and sainthood comparable to, if not more sophisticated than, medieval Europe. In the long, patient history of India's religions, the Christian message is in many respects but an awkward new arrival. One could assert that the Church in its approach to India has yet to come to grips with the wonderful depths and variety of the religious culture there which is perhaps as aware of its own value today as in the days of Francis Xavier or St Thomas.

Hence the theologian in India today has to pick his way among a variety of possible approaches. There exists the temptation to turn his back on past achievements in Church expansion—there are about ten million Christians in India, or about two per cent of the population, something like half of whom are Catholics—and give his whole attention to the masses of non-Christian India. He could turn his back on Roman and other imported liturgies to seek liturgical forms in Indian rites. So too he could dismiss as totally irrelevant the European theology and philosophy of his seminary days, and on the plea that the Church has developed no theology out of the fertile heritage of Hindu theology during nearly two thousand years, he could feel impelled to begin theologizing from scratch in Indian categories. Many suffer from the shock of post-colonial national resurgence which appears to challenge the well-bastioned European-style Catholic community they have long felt safe in; and the alternatives are to flee within the walls, or step out into the main-stream of national life. The radical, all-out approach which would jettison the past to begin afresh can bring much harm to the Church, but it surely offers more hope of new life for the Church in India than an embattled attitude seeking to preserve the faith in its foreign wrappings, be it from Jerusalem, Portugal or Rome. Salvation, it could be thought, lies in strengthening the existing Church against resurgent Hinduism, new Socialism, and the brash disdain for all tradition of the Marxists. For others it lies, to put it crudely, in joining the ranks of the opposition.

Such are some of the elements of the atmosphere in which a theologian in India must endeavour to ply his trade. And yet in the midst of this there is the great Hindu theological tradition which by and large has weathered with age but has retained its forms and influence over the people, an influence to which the Church until just recently has been all too securely insulated. Nevertheless, there are many theologians in India today who are attuned to the spiritual contribution Hinduism can make to the life of the Church, to the questions it raises in the fields of theology and pastoral practice. And there is generally a happy tendency to keep one foot in the past while determinedly stepping into the new path of the Indian tradition. The rest of this essay will attempt to elucidate some positive theological lessons being learned in this way.

I learned an unforgettable lesson in missionary methodology in the August of 1970, when I enrolled in Delhi University for research on Kabīr. I received notice through the post of my being assigned to an elderly, retired scholar as my director, and the same day called on him at his house. He received me at the door and invited me in. For an hour or more he treated me with the most compelling courtesy, encouraging me in my undertaking, introducing me to his family, insisting that his grand-daughter call me 'uncle', before he gently told me he had never heard of me until the moment I arrived at his door. And all the time I believed I had been expected! How different, I thought, from the bull-in-the-china-shop approach of the Church to non-Christian religions in the past! And it taught me to adopt a little of this troubador courtesy to the presence of God in India wherever and in whomsoever I should meet it.

In his *Evangelii Nuntiandi* Paul VI professes his great esteem for non-Christian religions, but at the same time calls attention to their incompleteness. With this one cannot disagree; but it would be less embarrassing to those in close contact with Hindus and Muslims if it were set beside the incompleteness of the Roman Catholic Church—we too are still far from the pleroma of Christ. The Pope's summing up of his argument on non-Christian religions is as follows: 'Our religion effectively establishes with God an authentic and living relationship which other religions do not succeed in doing, even though they have, as it were, their arms stretched out towards heaven'. This really says too little, and is unhappily worded. Behind the rhetoric of 'an authentic and living relationship' I presume is implied the grace of being taken into divine union, which, I think, can and does exist outside of the visible community of the Church. For I hold this as the first premise in an Indian theology: the word of God spoken by the Spirit to the hearts of men and through them to their society and culture, has preceded the arrival of the preaching Church. Hence the first thing to do is to be polite enough to listen and find out how far the conversation has progressed, so that one's contribution to it is not a rude butting in, engendering resentment, but will come in due course by invitation to join in.

A Christian then becomes a member of the household and not an intruder. This indispensable posture not only applies to the reading and study of the Indian religious tradition such as the *Upanishads,* the *Bhagavadgītā* or later devotional and theological literature, but also to personal contacts. One is after all dealing with the India of now, and saintliness in living Indians is the voice from the burning bush bidding one to respect hallowed ground. To depict a religious people as one with arms outstretched to heaven, but failing to achieve an authentic and living relationship with God, is to conjure up a picture of God teasing man to stretch out his hands in hunger and then withholding the bread.

THE STUDY OF KABĪR

The example of saintliness I have chosen is the fifteenth-century poet and mystic, Kabīr. He is an excellent illustration of the Indian religious achievement in so far as he not only is revered as a saint, studied as an important figure in early Hindi literature and probably the most quoted of Indian poets, but he is also something of a maverick in religious thought, standing aside as he does from the main sectarian traditions. And yet Kabīr is acclaimed by Hindus and Muslims alike as one of the great men of God of their history.

Kabīr is hard to classify, and to what extent his views are original or the result of a practical eclecticism is still disputed among scholars. The dispute begins in a sense from Kabīr's dates. The most commonly accepted date of his birth is 1398, though some would have him born almost half a century later. Then there is a popular tradition of his having died in 1518, extreme longevity being acceptable as one of the conventional marks of authenticity in Indian holy men. For a variety of reasons I am more inclined to locate the end of his life in the middle of the fifteenth century. This position automatically casts doubt on Kabīr's supposed discipleship of the great *bhakti*[1] teacher, Rāmānand, who is held to have died in 1410, and still more serious doubt on Kabīr's having instructed the founder of Sikhism, Nīnak, who was born only in 1469. This controversy over dates illustrates various approaches to Kabīr. Rāmānand is commonly held to have propagated devotion to Rām, the royal warrior *avatāra* of Vishnu, and hence Kabīr's discipleship of Rāmānand, if historically established, would lend weight to a theory of Kabīr's theology being similar to, and influenced by Rāmānand. However, some scholars now think that both Rāmānand and Kabīr could have, each in different ways, come under the influence of the Nāth movement, a branch of sectarian Yoga.

The rest of the more or less established information about Kabīr is a little sketchy. He was probably born in a family of weavers who some generations before would have been converted to Islam from their low position in the Hindu socio-religious structure. His name, Kabīr, a Koranic name meaning great, supports this hypothesis. He lived and died in or near Varanasi. He is included in a famous anthology of devotional poets, the *Bhaktamāla,* composed by Nābhādās at the end of the sixteenth century. Nābhādās identifies Kabīr as a poet whose verse expresses opposition to the philosophical and social tradition of Hinduism, and teaches a religion based on *bhakti*; he had a disregard for public opinion and propounded his simple non-conformist doctrine to Hindus and Muslims alike.

It is arguable that Kabīr owes to his Muslim background his strong sense of the uniqueness of God. On the other hand, this influence is not sufficient to explain his concept of God since in many of his mystical utterances he stands much closer to the non-dualism of *Vedānta.* Kabīr's first message to Islam is that love of God involves intimate union with God. However, the context of most of his verses addressed to Islam seems to be one of rather acrimonious controversy arising out of his attacks on the practices of Islam, such as summonses to public prayer in the mosque, circumcision and animal sacrifice. His clashes with the Qazis, or Islamic lawyers, on these issues, are perhaps symptomatic of the climate of anti-Islamic hostility in which he chose to live, aligning himself with the Hindu community against the social, religious and political aggression of Islam in the Sultanate of Jaunpur where he lived. For all this, however, I think it too jejune a view of Kabīr to see him principally as a renegade son of Islam. The evidence is strong that Kabīr's Islamic origins sat lightly on him, as also that, given our present knowledge of him, any attempt to classify him as a Sufi or one under Sufi influence cannot but appear as forced. In short, Kabīr speaks to the Islam of his time as a prophet from without the fold. He insisted above all on an interior religion without reference to rites, sacred places and the like. For instance the following line is among his milder anti-Islamic strictures: 'The one who enters into himself knows that this journey inwards is worth seventy pilgrimages to the Kaba' (*Pada* 184.6).[2] Holiness is for Kabīr an interior virtue without which there is no rapport with God, as he says in another polemical stanza: 'The unholy *(napak)* heart cannot recognize the holy *(pak),* and cannot grasp divine mysteries' (*Pada* 183.9). His antipathy to animal slaughter seems to be based on the very ancient Indian belief that 'every living thing is dear to the Lord' (*Pada* 186.8).

His insistence on the interiority of religion is probably the heart of Kabīr's teaching. Man must seek for God in his own heart and not in external rites or practices as he says in these oft quoted couplets: 'The deer searches the forest for the scent of the musk which all the time is coming from its own body; such is God's dwelling in each one's heart, but the worldly fail to see him. God is in your heart like the pupil in your eye; in their ignorance fools seek him outside of themselves' (*Sākhī* 7.1-2).

Kabir uses a variety of names for God which include names from Islam and the Hindu sects, though his favourite name for God, Rām, like a good number of other ones used by him, is of distinct vaishnavite origin. It is significant that in Dr Parasnath Tivari's critical text, *Kabīr Granthāvalī,* divine names of vaishnavite origin far outnumber all others. This shows his decided preference for the vaishnavite tradition, but it also complicates the problem of Kabīr's concept of God, because he denied the very basis of the vaishnavite concept of the divinity, the theory of *avatāra.* For just as Kabīr rejected the external rites of popular religion in favour of worshipping God in one's own heart, so too he dismissed as misleading the traditional belief in God's appearing in human form at various epochs in history. Thus the *avatāras,* Rām and Krishna, sacred images and sacred symbols alike are excluded from the practice of *bhakti.* In a vitriolic attack on such beliefs he says: 'Cling to that master who will support you and alleviate all joy and sorrow. He did not come down as an *avatāra* in Dasharatha's house . . . He did not come down as an *avatāra* in Devaki's womb . . . How could it be that he who is transcendent could have an earthly existence!' (*Ramainī* 3)

The key to understanding this attitude of Kabīr and many other aspects of his very individualistic religion is to see him as a yogi. Kabīr's verse is replete with the terminology of Yoga as it was practised by some of the sects of his time, notably the Nāths. The Nāth sect is popularly held to originate from the semi-legendary yogi, Matsyendranāth, thought to have lived in the tenth century. But the roots of the sect's chief tenets go back to classical Yoga as codified by Patanjali some centuries before the Christian era. Tantric Buddhism supplied some elements to a developing theory which had many practical manifestations, principally Hathayoga, whose principal exponent is held to be Svātmārāma in the twelfth century. The original insight announced by Patanjali: Yoga is the stilling of the activity of the mind (*citta vrtti nirodha*), was eventually married to the quasi-mystical physiology which bases all its psycho-somatic exercises on the supposition of a power (*śakti*) latent in every man, but awakened and brought to its flowering in wondrous experiences and powers by the accomplished yogi. In Kabīr's time at least two very different sects came to his attention, the Nāths to whom in many ways he is akin, and the Śāktas, or worshippers of *śakti,* whom he abhorred. Just how Kabīr came under the influence of the Nāths must remain a matter of conjecture, but while they, and especially Gorakhnāth, had no more admiring follower than Kabīr, he in fact turned their whole system from its native aims to his own purpose of reaching loving union with God. And so we have the best of Yoga asceticism such as its meditation technique, and the practice of rhythmic recitation of a name or a phrase, called *japa,* being adopted by this rebel prophet as a means of finding God, Rām, in his heart.

YOGA AND BHAKTI

It is part of the importance of Kabīr in our time that he consecrated yogic practice and domesticated it in a *bhakti* context. Nowadays Yoga and various adaptations of Indian meditational practices are being taught by genuine yogis and charlatans alike in many countries of the world. Even very laudable attempts have been made to base a Christian asceticism on the practices of Yoga, such as that of Dom Déchanet. Zen too, which owes something of its origin to ancient Indian ascetical techniques, has been taken out of its secular field and transplanted into the Church by such men as Hugo Makiba Enomiya Lassalle and William Johnston in Japan. In India Christian monasticism is seeking inspiration from the ashram tradition, and priests, religious and laity are doing the famous Goenka retreat, a rigorous course in a secularist and largely Buddhist asceticism. It is something often overlooked that the classical treatises on Yoga and the more popular sectarian expressions are in fact atheistic; they have no theology, and at best tolerate a postulate of *īśvara,* or supreme spirit, as a useful focal point of meditation. The Nāth sect seems to have been in practice equally atheistic. And so too is the popular form of Yoga being propagated throughout the world. Kabīr, on the contrary, constantly reminds us that the whole ascetical endeavour must debouch in an experience of God, and that yogic exercise and similar practices are but a means to this. The yogis are fond of the symbolism of the nectar said to flow from the inverted thousand-petalled lotus at the topmost point of the cranium. This is the symbol of yogic ecstasy. This mystical event takes place at the end of the long process of the reversal of all human faculties such as the working of the mind, which allows the otherwise dormant *śakti* to arise to its fulfilment. Kabīr uses this manner of speaking to his own end: 'My mind was inverted and found the flow (of nectar). But here are unfathomable depths which none can plumb, for Thou art the full depths of mercy' (*Sākhī* 9.33).

It is clear that Kabīr had experienced the loving embrace of God and was obsessed with it. For him this was the supreme ecstasy so much boasted of by the yogis. He turns frequently to nuptial imagery to express the joy of divine union, though this imagery, according to the classical Indian tradition, expresses both the happiness of union and the pain of separation from the beloved. In addition, for Kabīr divine love involves, one way or another, pain. He speaks of the pain of longing for God. But he also indicates that *bhakti* is of itself a painful experience: it is an arrow which pierces the heart, and none but the lover knows of this. He says: 'The love of Rām is a special arrow; only the one pierced knows the pain' (*Pada* 4.8). And yet the one whose lot it is to be so loved by God will nonetheless forsake all for such a boon.

This recalls another theme of Kabīr's, namely, the need for utter self-abandonment in finding divine love. *Bhakti* is the intoxicating liquor the price of which is the devotee's own head. The faithful widow casting herself on her husband's funeral pyre in her longing to be with him, is for Kabīr the image of the joyful and painful self-renunciation called for in divine love. Hence he often reminds men that it is not a common product easy to come by, but a precious diamond men must give all to buy, unconsciously echoing Jesus's own words.

Kabīr's *bhakti* is but another expression of the essence of Indian *bhakti* first expounded in the *Bhagavadgītā*, when Arjuna is instructed in it by the Lord, Bhagavan. This passage puts it most beautifully: 'And now give ear to this my highest word, of all the most mysterious: "I love you well." Therefore will I tell you your salvation. Bear Me in mind, love Me and worship Me, sacrifice, prostrate yourself to Me: so will you come to Me, I promise you truly, for you are dear to Me. Give up all things of law, turn to Me, your only refuge, for I will deliver you from all evils; have no care'. (*Bhagavadgītā* 18.64-66).[3] There in the polished serenity of Sanskrit verse is what Kabīr, perhaps two millennia later, is recalling his countrymen to. Kabīr's *bhakti* in turn is very little different in essence, though different in practice, from the ascetical counsel of *prapatti*, or total self-surrender in love, central to the theology of the tenth-century teacher, Rāmānuja, and later exponents of it such as Vallabha in the sixteenth century.

It is further noteworthy that Kabīr's *bhakti*, as distinct from Yoga and the path of knowledge of most *Vedānta* sects, has a place for a theory of divine grace. His prayers are simple and profound, such as this line: 'Hari, you are a mother to me and I am your child. Why should you not forgive my faults?' (*Pada* 37.1). In his longing to be finally united with God he cries: 'Kabir says: O Hari, grant this vision: either call me to yourself, or you yourself come to me' (*Pada* 47.5). He exclaims of the greatness of God's grace: 'Everything is done by the master, nothing by the servant: he can make a mountain out of a mustard seed, or turn a mountain into a mustard seed' (*Sākhī* 8.11).

Kabīr's practical witness to divine grace is echoed in the theologies of grace in the *bhakti* schools of both north and south India.

Such then is a glimpse of one important figure in the history of God's dealing with the people of India and of their response to his voice. Such a tangible proof of the presence of God's Spirit in the Indian tradition can scarcely be passed by, and surely furnishes a point of departure for an Indian theology, this time within the Christian community.

I was once asked by a pious Brahmin whether I considered Christianity to be primarily a *bhakti* religion, or after the manner of the *Vedānta,* to be a way of knowledge. I plumped for *bhakti,* not without some reservations. But why the question is so memorable is that I found myself in the position of letting India put the question, and was thus prodded into reading the gospels and reflecting on the Christian tradition to formulate an answer in Indian terminology. Others have answered the question differently. For instance, Sister Sarah Grant, RSCJ, has suggested that Christian mysticism can be considered Vedantine. Others have pondered whether Christian thought in India should lean more to Shankara's way of knowledge, or Rāmānuja's theology of *bhakti,* these two being the most eminent commentators on the *Bhagavadgītā.*[4] In any case they are doing what an Indian theology ought to do first of all, answer Indian questions.

Christian theology in India is in need of an ashram atmosphere where it can retire from the world field of theology, unruffled by the latest imports from Europe or anywhere else, and reflect on itself while listening to the voices of India speaking to it. Only in this way will it learn the right language, become sensitive to Indian categories of thought and expression, and the way God has chosen to reveal himself in India. We do not know what this will produce. Will we come to see the Church as something familiar to Indian eyes, for instance, Christ and God the Father as *gopāl,* or cowherd, in preference to the Semitic shepherd imagery? What term will emerge as most apt for the Holy Spirit, person and so on? Will Christ be endued safely with the term *avatāra,* as well as Incarnate God? Will the non-violent ethic of the Buddha take its place alongside the Gospel? How will the current flowering of developmental theology stand beside the traditional Indian ethic of detachment from the world? And above all, how will the full import of the Incarnation, Resurrection and the consequent consecration of the human and the created be married to an Indian soteriology which regards the flesh as an obstacle to divine grace and the world as ultimately unreal? These are some of the questions for the Christian theologian in the ashram. And meantime he will be in good company with Kabīr and many living Indians touched by the love of God.

Notes

1. The transliteration of Indian language words is here adjusted in spelling and the use of diacritics to aid pronunciation, and not according to any scientific system. The word *ashram*, literally 'absence of labour', means a place of refuge from worldly activity, a hermitage.

2. My own translation from Parasanath Tivari's text, *Kabīr Granthāvalī* (Allahabad, 1961). There are three main verse forms: the *Pada,* or stanza, the *Ramainī,* a stanza of another metrical tradition, and the *Sākhī,* or couplet. There is a good English translation of the *Sākhī* verses in Ch. Vaudeville, *Kabir I* (Oxford, 1974), based largely on Tivari's text.

3. The translation is that of R. C. Zaehner, *The Bhagavad-Gita* (Oxford, 1969).

4. See, Sarah Grant RSCJ, 'Swamiji: the Man', in *Clergy Monthly,* 38 (1974), pp. 487-95. See also Sarah Grant, 'Reflections on the Mystery of Christ Suggested by a Study of Sankara's Concept of Relation', in G. Gispert-Sauch, SJ, ed., *God's Word Among Men* (Delhi, 1973), pp. 105-16. Abhishiktananda's own views are in his *Saccidananda: A Christian Approach to Advaitic Experience* (Delhi, 1974).

Jean-Pierre Jossua

Changes in Theology and its Future

THE PRESENT *Concilium* dedicated to the changes that have taken place in theology over the last ten years has no editorial. This was intentional. We didn't want the individual pieces—selected from among many others we also could have published—to be introduced by a global interpretation which might in fact take a culturally restricted point of view not acceptable to all. During the discussion at the *Concilium* general assembly held at Chantilly in 1976, in which this theme was raised, some colleagues had difficulty with the term 'displacement' or 'transformation'. As it couldn't be a linguistic barrier, we wondered whether it was the concept itself which was causing the trouble, or whether some of us had really tried to implement a change which was much more radical than a development along the same lines, and some had not. Some of the delegates' failure to understand was all the more surprising, because we had devoted the first two days of the assembly to a round-table discussion during which each of us told the others what had changed in his work since the foundation of the journal. The metaphor of 'displacement': not being in the same place where you were before, being 'somewhere else' seemed to me the only suitable word for what all these very different accounts had in common—to mention only a few: van Iersel, Gutierrez, Merino, Greinacher, Pohier, Floristan and Baum. However, even in France the term required three conferences to clarity it, in Paris, Lyon and Strasbourg in 1976-7.

The number which this article closes, rather than concluding it, shows without any possible doubt the fact that during the last twelve years the changes that have happened have been much more radical than during the period preceding Vatican II, which this Council ratified. I want to try to give a general outline of these changes, at my own risk, and of course all generalization involves risk. I shall also risk, without claiming any special gifts as a seer or prophet, a guess at the way theology will go in the future if it continues along the same lines.

THEOLOGY 'MOVES'

The starting point: the theology of 'renewal'

As I said, when we speak of 'displacement' or 'moving house' in theology we mean something much more than a deepening or discovery of new implications in research, or even a shift of interest common in all academic life. Neither is it just that new dominant themes have replaced those of the previous period, and that a period of intense interest in the Church has been succeeded by another in which every self-respecting theologian has written a Christology and a commentary on the creed. New fashions such as radical theology, death-of-God theology, theologies of hope or liberation, charismatic or neo-Byzantine theologies, do not as such amount to a 'displacement' which affects the very nature of theological activity, and involves questions about working methods, reference systems, a way of life, and the total human experience of theologians.

As a contrast, but also as supportive evidence, because 'displacement' is also partly a prolongation of these changes, I shall quickly run through the 'renewals' brought about by the Council which dominate the prevalent theology in the Church today. Of course traces remain of a more archaic period, particularly in official documents, and we also see the mark of pre-conciliar theology in many areas such as the continued usage of scholastic-type categories, references to 'natural' law or morality, the apologetic stance taken in recourse to biblical documents or the history of early Christianity. These tendencies are still at work in the power structure of the Church but in its intellectual life they are really no more than a discredited left-over. On a world-wide scale the dominant theology is the theology called 'conciliar', the theology of renewal developed partly in secret over the last thirty years and finally accepted as official by the Church authorities.

There is no need to describe this renewal in detail. There is the biblical renewal, the joyful rediscovery of the vigour of the Old Testament and the freshness of the Gospel which go beyond mere hermeneutics, the discovery of a 'biblical theology' uniting various authors on one theme or another and relegating a discredited scholasticism to the attic. There is the liturgical renewal: the rediscovery and revivification of the creative periods of the Christian liturgy and the ancient theologies that went with them. There is the patristic renewal: a return to the sources of the Fathers of the Church (who were so down to earth and so pastoral) and more research into the living presence of this tradition in current theology. There is the ecumenical renewal: the joy in meeting and respecting other believers, friendly theological discussions with them—each speaking from the point of view of his own Church—in the hope of slowly drawing closer together. There is the 'missionary' renewal, particularly within the Western Christian world which is becoming de-Christianized, and thinking about the meaning of 'mission'. There is an opening-up to the collective and historical dimension of human existence. And there is the discovery of modern, especially existential, philosophies.

All this was a great step forward, and one full of promise which would seem enough to be going on with for many years to come. *Concilium* itself was founded on this hope. In fact, as I said, this theology of 'renewal' is still going on: it dominates seminaries all over the world; it is the theme of a flood of books and periodicals aimed at the Christian public. But quite quickly—and we find signs of it in the last fifty numbers of *Concilium*—other developments appeared. They quickly turned out to be fundamental and their effect on theology was to shake its certainty and unity and give it the feel it was groping rather than asserting. It was much more than 'renewal'. This new development was not a simple phenomenon that could be neatly categorized; things were changing in all directions, and the only metaphor fit to describe it was that of 'displacement'.

OVER A CRITICAL THRESHOLD

The first displacement that I should mention is known to all intellectually active theologians. Even those who are doubtful about the term have been forced to recognize it, and to a greater or lesser extent accept it or promote it. It is also the most spectacular and public: a widespread anxiety about matters of faith betrays its influence or the fact that it could be the theoretical and theological expression of a development common to a large number of Christians.

This move was a continuation of 'renewal', change after change, but this time following a logic that had not been foreseen. We could say that all the research that had been done, which up to that point has been essentially positive, accumulated results which overstepped a critical threshold. It would be truer to say that it had come back to the critical threshold that had been reached at the end of the last century, which had been systematically denied by the repression of 'Modernism'. The Protestants, at least in biblical matters, had reached this point at least a century and a half earlier. It was only too easy to mock at their absurdities and their schisms. What they had to pay for,

Catholic theology took advantage of: without the results they had achieved, one might well wonder what sort of a mess faith in the Church would be in today.

Let us go through the recent 'renewals' one by one. The rediscovery of 'biblical' theology was succeeded by the period of 'exegesis': historical criticism without doctrinal prejudices, the creation of theologies of the New Testament, endless problems of hermeneutics and its criteria. The enthusiasm of the liturgical renewal was succeeded by a period of fundamental reflection on the cult and the sacred, during which it was realized that it is easier to restore than to create and the disappointment caused by the liturgical movement, instead of the expected delight, had to be painfully analyzed. Pleasure in the rediscovery of doctrinal tradition was succeeded by the painful awareness of its diversity, its anachronistic character, its variations in time, and the difficulty of setting up historical frontiers between 'orthodoxy' and 'heresy'. In the ecumenical movement polite official discussions gave way to common research by theologians or local groups on the basis of an agreed common Christianity which was often considered as sufficient. Finally the burst of 'missionary' activity within the old Christian countries—the discovery of unbelief, the efforts to organize to communicate the faith—has died down: it had to be admitted that the obstacles were insurmountable and an attempt made to analyze what it was in the Christianity being preached or the cultural situation of the people the message was offered to, that had led to such a failure.

So many changes, so many problems! And this was still fairly familiar ground. This was still just one more development of religion, although perhaps an exceptionally radical one.

THE ARRIVAL OF MODERNITY

A second type of displacement, which perhaps has not been so widely popularized but is more original and more crucial, is not a prolongation of anything, but completely new. Modernity is at last making its way into Christian thinking. Theologians are using, either as instruments or as reference points, new disciplines in their theological work. These new disciplines, both practical and theoretical, are not only outside the traditional Christian field or the practice of the Church, but also difficult or impossible for Christianity to digest—the same thing happened long ago, for example with Greek 'philosophy'. These new disciplines are still too hot for theologians to handle, even though they represent all the last century and a half's efforts to understand and make sense of mankind's most fundamental problems. Of course there had previously been 'dialogues' with 'outsiders', a 'going out into the world'—which was at least something. But the meeting always took place too late between Christians and militant atheists defensively entrenched in their positions. The new style of relationship is completely different.

So what happens, when theology abandons its introversion and goes out to meet psychoanalysis (or psychology as a whole), sociology, linguistics (and modern thought on language and writing), ethnology, the science of religions? When the theologian is also acquainted with these other disciplines? Or when theology arises from within political practice or artistic creation? Or even when the theologian abandons his tame philosophy and history and tries to consort with the philosophers and historians of the day? His theology is bound to be deeply affected in its interests, methods and stumbling-blocks. And these modifications will not present a united or coherent statement, as we see from the example of the articles in this *Concilium*.

THE DEBUNKING OF THEOLOGIANS AND THE EXPLOSION OF THEOLOGY

These removals or shifts I have mentioned imply many under-lying social phenomena. Let us review the change in social or ecclesiastical status of the theologians themselves. The rather vulgar word 'debunking' seems to me appropriate to describe their new distance from clerical status, academic life, pleasure in systematic thought, and dependence on church authorities.

First, the academic teaching of theology has been greatly reduced in certain countries, with the disappearance of many seminaries. Theologians who were once university teachers or teachers of future priests have often become teachers of theology to the laity, who are very critical and sometimes become theologians themselves, or group leaders of priests, religious or laity. No doubt this is an attempt on the part of the theologians to regain a social platform—as one of the articles in this number shows—but do they do it simply because they have no choice and with no will to serve? Furthermore theologians are often obliged to earn their living by doing other work as well as theology, a 'worldly' job. This involves important changes in their methods and interests which are of course related to the second displacement mentioned above.

And for the same reason another displacement has taken place whose importance should not be disregarded. There is often a move away from the primacy of systematic reflection, theology worked out in large tomes to works based on experience, an investigation and criticism of 'faith as it is experienced', of common Christian life. This new polarization is inseparable both as means of investigation and expression, from an awareness of literary form, style, and even the attempts at poetry which are intended to be authentically theological. Thus the most interesting theological products in recent years—apart from a few great Christologies—have all been essays. They are written in the first person, or at least in a very personal style, speak from experience and appeal to the reader's own experience, forcing him to consider what is being said personally and agree or disagree. These essays help to create a new language of faith which would—were it not for the problem of religious book distribution especially in Latin countries—reach a wider public, as well as acquiring, through the very effort of writing this type of work, a new kind of rigour. Of course this type of research, together with the diversity of current trends and the differing political positions, accentuate the plurality of theologies today.

Finally we should mention a general change of attitude among theologians towards official ecclesiastical texts, especially when these lay claim to universality. It is becoming rarer that theologians consider it their duty—as most of them did before the Council—to explain, support and circulate these texts. It is even rare for theological work to be based on them. At any rate—and perhaps this also applies to some extent to tradition and Scripture—when theologians use these texts they use them as reference points rather than authorities. In a broader sense we could say that theology tends now to be done by people living as members of the Church rather than in institutions. Of course the crucial matter here is moral theology. The gap between the actual practice of Christians in many things and particular in sexual matters, and the official language of the Church has brought about a double crisis. There is the crisis of authority of course, but also the crisis of moral theology as a science of norms which is losing face. Theological thought on this development is much more hesitant, seeking rather to understand what is happening with some resort to the Gospel, than to pronounce universal rules claiming to be invariable.

Perhaps this debunking of theologians is the greatest contributor to the instability of the international theological community and the key to the differences that are appearing among theologians according to their education, situation and attitudes. There has been a very surprising regionalization. Instead of becoming more universal, as we expected (international reviews like *Concilium* were created with this end in view), theology has become more and more particularized according to local cultures, which are finding it increasingly difficult to communicate with one another. At international meetings, or in periodicals, we cannot escape the impression that with rare exceptions of blocks such as the Germans and Dutch, the North Americans, Latin Europe (to which France has come closer), the Latin Americans are speaking a different language, to say nothing of the Asians and Africans whose voice as yet is barely heard but who will be in the near future, as the 'Manifesto of Dar-es-Salaam' forcefully made clear. The 'human sciences' and political consciousness are very different in these different places. Social developments and the change in the professional status of theologians sometimes also produce an even simpler dichotomy: Germans and North Americans *versus* Latins and Latin Americans. Will we soon have a theology for the rich and a theology for the poor?

WHAT WILL THEOLOGY BE LIKE TOMORROW?

This rapid change has not yet been assimiliated by the majority of Christian people, or by the Church officials with their official theologians, or by whole countries which have remained more traditional. Should we project it into the future and draw a hypothetical graph going further in the same direction stating that this is what theology will be like tomorrow? Not necessarily. Unexpected factors might upset our graph, and new, even more radical changes might occur. Or there could be a strong reaction in the opposite direction, as there was during the 'Modernist' period. Then we would see a pleiad of Lefebvres, impeccably Roman, assembling a—considerably reduced—group of 'true believers' and their thinkers would reinterpret current changes as decadence and heresy. But, apart from these two extreme possibilities, we can try to say something about the future in the light of what is happening now. It will not be a harmonious picture of convergence, but simply an attempt to discern, amid the variety and the disagreements, some points which will become the crucial ones.

1. We will no longer be able to use theological language with innocent abandon as if this usage presented no problems, and we certainly won't be able to build complicated systems founded on bold confidence in 'reason'. The psychological and social functions of speaking and writing, the metaphysics implicit in naive usage of theological language, the crazy character of the vast theological edifices, will make this plain to all—unless the wind changes.

However, this will not mean another reincarnation of anti-intellectualism, simplicism, pietism and fundamentalism. Reason will not be banished from faith and will still be accepted as ineluctable, with faith's human health and truth depending on a constant measuring up against it.

2. No theology will be constructed without being founded on human experience, the experience of believers, or at least constantly tested against it. No theologian will write behind a barrier of 'objectivity' but will have to try to regain the personal and speak from within himself. No religious author will put pen to paper without bothering about style:

the job of writing, the original effort required in the act of creation to link two distant minds who do not know each other. No Christian thinking will be based on a past or present text claimed to be a sacred, absolute, intangible norm. They will go to the text for inspiration and their interpretation of it will be an attempt to say something new.

But witness is not all. This modest, free, conscientious individual or group work of theology will come face to face with all kinds of criticism which derive from a new view of mankind. The new theology must examine the source of its desire for God, and make sure that the speaker can say 'I' without being merely naive. The writer must check his Christian identity against Christian practice, and seek a unity in the varieties of Christian experience. He must ensure that any experience or meaning is communicable and transmissible to others.

3. In the future the meeting between faith and the various aspects of modernity will consist more in personal dialogue rather than in confrontation between an established Christian practice or knowledge and a 'world' known too late, from the outside. The psychoanalyst or patient whose faith remains after treatment or, as can happen, is discovered during treatment, the revolutionary who still finds the Gospel has something to say in the heat of the struggle, will speak from their own experience, not as Christian 'specialists' in Marx or Freud who are clever at bookish discussions.

We have come to a crossroads and are faced with a terrible dilemma. What will be the outcome? A new religion of the future derived from Christianity, having taken from the New Testament and tradition what suits it? Or an entirely secular world, a-religious, for which Christian striving remains a provocation and unavoidable question in its own search for self-transcendence? Or, more classically, a reinterpretation of the essential message of the New Testament, without sacrificing even the 'unbelievable': continuing a tradition which has coped with many such re-readings? Furthermore it is not easy to decide what this 'essential' is, and we are all conservatives or demolishers in others' eyes.

4. The final point is the social aspect. It will no longer be possible to forget that all discourse is produced in a certain context and that—even if we avoid the over-simplification of talking about 'superstructures' and 'reflections'—it is to some extent the product of this context. All theology bears the mark of its socio-political (university, bourgeois, rich country) and socio-ecclesial (clergy or laity, belonging or not to a certain group, authorized or not by the hierarchy, and so on) provenance. If we forget or deny this, we are dupes and also mystifiers of others. Theology will require a criticism of theology from this point of view, with refined methods.

But must theology be nothing but a criticism of theology? What has been called 'political theology' over the last few years sometimes seemed like it, as if it remained in the 'camp' simply in order to 'break it up'.

Of course, as one article in this number shows, criticism takes a totalizing viewpoint, lets nothing past. But must it also therefore be totalitarian, excluding any other approach? That is the question. There are also newer forms of this kind of self-destruction: circles which only talk about Christianity in order to tear it to pieces, discussions in which 'questioning' has completely ousted 'affirmation'. Why bother if Christianity no longer has anything positive to offer? What is the point of squeezing a few last drops out of a Bible which has been bled dry by historical materialism, if the spiritual river which Judaeo-Christianity was no longer waters any living crops?

5. That is why Christian theology will not exist tomorrow unless it arises anew from intense spiritual experience. It must not fear to go on with the endless search for God and to welcome his manifestation in Jesus Christ (which is its true message), to be aware of the outpourings of the Spirit. It will not despise the other religious experiences of mankind by calling them 'natural', will not reduce them to what it already knows, will not dismiss them as 'opium'—while being fully aware that they too can alienate as well as Christianity. It will listen to them, offer them what it has to offer, let them be what they are, and borrow from them things which do not clash with Christian beliefs. It will spend more effort in seeking out hidden sources, and be as interested in forgotten secrets as in the latest discoveries.

But it will do this without credulity, occultism, spiritualism, para-psychology, glossolalia, palmistry, macrobiotics, theosophy, Gnosticism, incense, bio-energetics, fundamentalism and ingnorantism. It will not ignore criticism, it will not be apolitical, it will not be idealist (we are solid bodies after all!), it will not go in for astrology (even if it is 'scientifically' re-accredited) or Jungism, Clavelism, or Neo-Byzantine stereotypes.

6. Tomorrow there will not be a theology as there used to be, there will not even be several western theologies, corresponding to different spiritual families, as there are today. There will be many different theologies, throughout the world, corresponding to different cultures and deep roots, with different hopes for the future. Their emphases, their situations, their principal spokesmen will be different and accepted as such: they will read Christian tradition differently, and the will approach it differently.

This blossoming forth of many theologies will present grave problems for the unity of the faith. What can unity mean in these circumstances? Or will it be above them? Perhaps it will be a bit like the persistence of a substantially identical Christian message throughout its continual historical reinterpretations. Faith has existed throughout history but can only be found in its historical embodiments, not as some pure 'essence' outside history. Likewise, in its modern geographical diversity, faith will not be an isolated chemical element, but recognizable within all these different embodiments. Every community—whatever historically separated Church it has derived from, because they will all get back all the cards—will assert that what any other community proclaims, is what it also believes, within its differences. But there will also be problems of unity in the actual, social interpretation of the Gospel. Diversity can be accepted, even political. But can straight contradiction be accepted indefinitely? Racialism and anti-racialism, for example? A reading of the beatitudes as an invitation (to oneself) to become a maker of justice, peace and brotherhood or as an obligation (for others) to accept consolation only in the hereafter?

In future theology will no longer be clerical. It will be worked out by groups of Christians, at the 'base'. It will be the expression of their experience—particularly in areas in which the clergy used to make the rules without bearing the consequences—and of their reading of the Gospel. The research and reflection of many lay people, historians, journalists, philosophers, writers and poets, already in existence, will be fully recognized. The ministers themselves will be de-clericalized, chosen in the community without being separated from it, and this will modify their theological work. If there are full-time theologians, they will be at the service of the common task.

For this to happen several problems will have to be solved which as yet have hardly been raised. There can be no serious thinking without education, which at the moment is not being given. This becomes obvious when you have worked often for a long time with lay groups, tried to invite them to work out a formulation of their faith, a theology of their own, to become aware of their potential and the poverty of the means at present at their disposal. This education must be invented, and must go much further than timid efforts to transmit clerical knowledge. Moreover there can be no theological thinking at the base, taken from experience, if it is not supported by more intellectually rigorous research. Who will engage in it? How will they be trained? Who will support them financially? So many hopes, so much to be done.

Have I read the signs correctly? Does my picture of the future ring true or false? The different replies to these two questions will at least prove, I am sure, my principal point: theology has moved so far that its unity has exploded.

Translated by Dinah Livingstone

Contributors

KLAUS AHLHEIM was born in Saarbrücken, Germany, in 1942. He studied Protestant theology, sociology and education. He is a student chaplain in Frankfurt am Main. He has published on social ethics, political theology and problems of church education.

ALFREDO BARDAJÍ was born in Soria, Spain, in 1936. He is qualified in theology, clinical psychology and civil law. He is director of the Madrid University Institute of Theology and director of publications of the Spanish Federation of Societies for the Protection of the Mentally Handicapped. He has published widely on faith, Christianity and Socialism, religious language and pastoral questions.

FRANÇOIS BUSSINI was born at Sallanches, France, in 1936 and is a priest of the Besançon diocese. He has taught fundamental theology at the Catholic faculty of Strasbourg University since 1970. He is the author of a major work on man as a sinner and has written many articles on the local church.

KARL DERKSEN was born in Emmerich in 1937. He is a Dominican and teaches in Utrecht. He is also a theological assistant in the Dominican parish in Amsterdam and has published widely on the religious life, Christianity and Socialism, solidarity and the basic community movement.

WILLIAM DWYER is the senior Hindi teacher at St. Xavier's School, Bokaro Steel City. He was born in Melbourne in 1930, joined the Society of Jesus in 1948 and has been in India since 1952. He has published a book on Kabir's concept of the love of God and is still engaged in Kabir studies while lecturing at the faculty of Asian studies, Australian National University, in a part-time capacity.

ELISABETH SCHÜSSLER FIORENZA was born in 1938 in Tschanad, Rumania. She studied theology at Würzburg and Münster, was guest professor at Union Theological Seminary, New York, and since 1970 has been professor of New Testament studies at the University of Notre Dame, Indiana, USA. She has published on women in the Church, the priesthood and the Apocalypse, and religious propaganda in Judaism and early Christianity.

JEAN-PIERRE JOSSUA, O.P., was born in 1930 at Boulogne-sur-Seine, France. He studied medicine in Paris, and theology at the Saulchoir faculties and at Strasbourg. He is a lecturer in theology and has been a professor at the Saulchoir faculty since 1965 and at the Institut Catholique de Paris since 1971. Among his publications are studies of liturgy, salvation, and Christianity as a religion of the masses or the élite.

JEAN-PIERRE LECONTE was born in 1936. He has been a priest in the Autun diocese since 1963 and is director of the theology and religious science seminar at the Institut Catholique de Paris. He is also a research sociologist.

TIEMEO RAINER PETERS was born in Hamburg in 1938. He studied at the Dominican seminary at Walberberg, Bonn, Germany and at Münster University. He is scientific assistant in the Catholic theology department of Münster University.

ANDRÉ ROUSSEAU was born in France in 1941. He was attached to the socio-religious research centre of Louvain University for some years. Since 1972 he has taught at the Institut Catholique de Paris. He is researching into French Catholicism. He has published on the reactions of religious institutions during revolutionary crises, and Jews in catechesis.

FUMIO TABUCHI was born at Kobe, Japan, in 1935. He studied at Sophia University, Tokyo. From 1970 to 1977 he was guest lecturer in systematic theology and philosophical anthropology at the same university. He has translated Metz, Ratzinger and Rahner and has edited two Catholic journals.

BAS VAN IERSEL was born at Heerlen, the Netherlands, in 1924. He was ordained in 1950. He studied at Nijmegen and Louvain universities. He teaches NT studies at Nijmegen, edits two theological journals and has published exegetical studies.